If you're considering whether cultural development needs to be part of your business strategy you need this book. Not only will it give you compelling reasons why culture matters, it will ask you the deeper questions about the actions you take and how you want to be known as an employer. This practical toolkit will help you build a better future for your business and your employees.

Lucy Adams, CEO Disruptive HR

Culture is the golden thread that weaves customer expectations into employee actions. Leanne offers thoughtful insights and relevant tools to create the right culture so that employees can better fulfil their potential. Any leader embarking on a culture journey can use the ideas in this book as a blueprint for action.

Dave Ulrich
Rensis Likert Professor, Ross School of Business,
University of Michigan
Partner, The RBL Group

The Golden Thread challenges the reader to think carefully about how to create the target culture for their organization and provides practical steps on creating and embedding culture to build solid business success. A light-hearted, quick read on a topic highly relevant to business today.

Lara Spencer
Formerly at DHL – VP Human Resources

T0150989

Packed with both theory and practical insight, there are so many thought starters in this book that no matter where you stand on your company culture, there will be relevant areas that you'll want to take action on – and your head will be buzzing with the potential for more! Be prepared for a whole raft of questions that will help you uncover and creatively develop the culture in your business – right from the very first chapter.

Nikki Gatenby
Founder, NED; Coach
Author of the bestseller Superengaged

Culture and the principles shared within this book resonate across all industries including the sporting world. Time and effort spent shaping the culture of teams can be the difference between winning and losing. Leanne captures a full range of considerations and tools that can be put into action to support the development and ambition of any team.

Paul Telfer
Ex Premier League footballer – Coventry City,
Southampton and Celtic

A thought-provoking journey that challenges the reader to think again about what they know and understand about culture development. Whether public or private sector, there is a vast amount to learn from the 'golden thread' that runs through this book.

On a personal note, when leading large teams through complex, protracted, often traumatic investigations into serious crime, the approach I have learnt from *The Golden Thread* will pay dividends for my teams. It provides subtle yet vitally important considerations that underpin any team's objectives.

Steve Taylor
Detective Chief Superintendent (retired)

The right culture in your business is key to meeting customer expectations and also helping employees achieve their full potential. *The Golden Thread* gives practical examples of how to best assess your culture and also how to improve it to better achieve your goals. Extremely well written, and having worked with Leanne for a number of years, I can verify that *The Golden Thread* encompasses her own beliefs and culture philosophy completely.

Mike Dunn
Retired Vice President – logistics industry

Building an effective culture is a leader's most critical and challenging task. *The Golden Thread* de-bunks the myths and provides a clear roadmap for how you can build and sustain a culture that will ensure your teams stay ahead of the competition.

Chris Hirst
Global CEO, Creative Havas

There are a lot of business growth and leadership books in the marketplace that cover a wide range of subjects. *The Golden Thread* focuses in on what is for me the most crucial area of business and leadership, culture! Leanne not only gives you a forensic-like analysis of the key areas of success and failure; she also provides the knowledge, behaviours and tools to move you forward in your pursuit of developing a high-performance culture within your organization. Not only will this book support the growth of your business; it will allow you to give it a heartbeat.

Luke Hall
Managing Director, PTI Worldwide Limited

Culture is a topic that is often talked about but poorly defined and executed. *The Golden Thread* helps demystify organizational culture and provides some simple, practical but highly effective examples of how to identify, assess and develop your desired culture. The book walks you through the steps to take in a way that enables you to take action immediately and start your journey to the culture you desire. A great guide to help you achieve your goals, how you want to achieve them.

Andrew Gibb, COO – Healthcare

THE GOLDEN THREAD

How consistent culture creates purposeful people and high performance

LEANNE HAMLEY

First published in Great Britain by Practical Inspiration Publishing, 2021

© Leanne Hamley, 2021

The moral rights of the author have been asserted.

ISBN   9781788602662 (print)
       9781788602655 (epub)
       9781788602648 (mobi)

Practical Inspiration
Publishing

Contents

Foreword

Business leaders have a responsibility to purposefully design and consistently live their culture – fact! It cannot be left to chance: the repercussions of a toxic and damaging culture are catastrophic to employees, customer experience, public perception and quite frankly bottom-line profitability.

The Golden Thread unpacks the science behind great organizational cultures; it shuns theory in favour of real, evidence-based tools, practices and metrics that once implemented *will* deliver results. Leanne's career working for organizations of varying industries and size allow her to highlight the key challenges and opportunities as seen with her own eyes, from the front line to the board room. Her knowledge of the elements that organizations who 'get it right' live and breathe every day shine through this book on each and every page.

Depending on where you are at currently with your organizational culture, it can feel an insurmountable task to take on. Fear not! Leanne expertly holds your hand while navigating every twist and turn of your cultural strategy. Breaking it down into bite-size manageable actions, Leanne provides a practical blueprint for you to follow. Her passion for great organizational culture is palpable and it's her pull-no-punches style of writing that is refreshingly challenging and thought provoking. While written with a huge dose of humour, the message is not lost; this is a real problem for many organizations and Leanne does not sugar coat any of it.

Delivered with an abundance of personality, Leanne rejects the tick-box exercises of cultural strategy seen in so many businesses today and offers simplified, humanized, proven tools to build or enhance your organization's culture!

If you are unable to have Leanne actually consult with you in your business, then this book is the next best thing.

Kate Bowers
People & Performance Director at Pti Worldwide

Introduction

If you're reading this book, then you are probably questioning whether the culture of your organization is the right one to lead your business in the direction you want it to go. To meet that purpose, this book has been written to provide you with greater context as to why culture in business is critical to organizational success.

The analogy of the *golden thread* is a metaphor. One that runs through each page and will provide a visual to the full span of culture. This book will provide you with tools, guidance and questions for you to review the impact of your existing culture and considerations to shape your target culture, one that improves profitability to the bottom line and to the environment you curate for your employees to thrive. When it's a great culture you can feel it, you can see it, it's in the eyes of everyone around you. There's a buzz, because everyone is pulling in the same direction and results are being outperformed. When it's not great, then the culture can be toxic – disgruntled employees who don't want to be there, everything takes longer, politics gets in the way... it can be mind-blowingly business damaging. It will eat away at the profits, the leaders and the employees. Because of the culture, leaders will find more and more ways of hiding the spiralling costs. There is a commercial impact. Toxic cultures impact your bottom line.

But the damage of a poor culture isn't just the spiralling costs. The impact is far greater: it's the brand damage, the loss of customers; it's the bitterness shared within each interaction of your employees; it's the tears shared before a day in the office or the anxiety brought home each evening. It's the time taken to rebuild after significant change has been imposed on your people.

And how do we know that? Well, the true test of culture is crisis. At the time of writing, we are in the middle of a global pandemic; it's not the first, and it might not be the last – a paradigm-shifting worldwide crisis. How did your business respond? Was your business one that responded in a way that instilled pride in your employees, one that showed empathy and transparency in its actions? Or was it one where the raw nature of the culture was exposed – profit over people? Survival over extinction?

Whilst organizations with toxic cultures will see the negative outcomes of that culture spiral during a crisis, organizations with strong cultures bounce back from a crisis quicker. The culture is already shaped and measures are in place to track the impact, resulting in a culture strong enough to overcome the challenges.

There is hope. Cultural action can be taken. It's not how hard we fall, but how quick we are to get back up that counts. And don't worry, this is not a human resources mutiny! Far from being the remit of 'just the HR department', culture and cultural development should be driven by the collective board. A board which understands that the better the culture is, the better the profitability of the organization, as well as having a moral obligation to employee wellbeing.

Now is the time to recognize that with every action you take – in business and in life – there is an intention. So what's your intention in how you choose to treat your employees? Do they work for you? Do they work for the organization? Where is their loyalty placed? As they serve you in their role, is the role of every manager or leader to also serve them reciprocally? And for the organization to have created the environment, the right culture and the right development to make that happen?

It's time to lead a new agenda. One which doesn't see culture as a delimited project, but as an ongoing part of who we want this business to become. It is a way of life; and in the work context, it's 'how we do things around here'. Cultural development needs to be an ongoing priority of the business, one that is measured, continually reviewed and enhanced. This book has been shaped to simplify what can be seen as a complex theory and provide some practical steps in breaking down culture into chunks. In the following pages, we will explore the intrinsic links between behaviour, data and process, to strategy and results. To untangle the thread is to understand the current culture, and as we delve into each thread you will have the opportunity to identify any chinks in your cultural armour. Better still, you'll have the chance to see the potential for small, employee-led changes. Where organizations commit to strengthening the thread that binds... then the output is truly golden.

Happy reading!

1

The golden thread of culture explained

To write about culture, we must first address strategy and leadership. Some leaders bandy the word 'strategy' around like some magical panacea – thinking that the word will endow them with protection due to its elusive nature. The overused and misused term 'strategy' needs some clarification. Strategy is a set of actions designed to achieve a long-term or overall goal.

When we are talking about culture, we need a plan that is aligned to the overall business strategy. Cultural shaping cannot be completed without first understanding the long-term goal the business is trying to achieve.

To design and execute strategy you need leadership. Both strategy and leadership, in whatever form, should be visible to those being led.

Culture, however, is harder to grasp. Culture, unless clearly defined, is anchored into the unspoken actions, behaviours and mindset of those employed. What is not challenged becomes the acceptable form of culture. An unconscious culture is one where leaders do not deliberately and thoughtfully set the culture. Instead, how they lead automatically becomes the culture itself. Maybe you can recognize some of these examples from places you have visited or worked: the turning of a blind eye to poor behaviour because it gets results; the erratic and voluminous emails flying every which way; the direction in the whole company – or lack of it. These are behaviours that, when replicated top-down, create an environment which is claustrophobic and limiting.

Or maybe, the organization *has* defined a culture. There is a clear statement of values artfully emblazoned on every wall of the office... but the day-to-day behaviour of the people in that office doesn't match up. If the behaviours and the stated culture are misaligned, the behaviour will override and determine the culture. This too is how a defined culture can unravel.

A conscious culture, on the other hand, is one where the culture is defined, along with the leadership style – and those two things are congruent! Furthermore, the behaviour of both leadership and employees are aligned as well. Then you have a hallelujah moment, and a healthy, self-sustaining culture!

Established theory

This is not an academic textbook. It's not about understanding the theory and ignoring the practice, and the majority of the following chapters will focus on pragmatic steps for cultural development. However, a theoretical grounding is important in establishing good practice, so it is key to look briefly at the academic research around what culture is, and the research into the types of culture and how they originate.

Edgar Schein's Model of Organization Culture

Edgar Schein, renowned professor of the MIT Sloan School of Management, studied extensively in the field of organizational management. In 2004 Schein developed the 'Model of Organizational Culture'.[1] Schein pointed out that for a culture to be shaped, we first must understand how a culture

---

[1] E. Schein, *Organizational Culture and Leadership.* Nicholas Brealey Publishing Ltd., 2004.

arises. Groups of people can determine the culture because they have history, have grown together, solved problems together, and won or grown the business together. New people may have joined and challenged legacy behaviours, and along the way the culture may have changed because of it, but the organization is already entrenched in a set way.

In Schein's research, he proposed that organizational cultures were built on three factors:

1. *Artefacts*: This is the visible culture, clothing, office space, technology and communications.
2. *Values*: These are the 'espoused' values, the documented company's values (e.g. the values printed in huge letters on the wall!).
3. *Basic assumptions*: These are the actions people take; for example, the volunteering of a new idea or concept, or the lack of sharing it for fear of putting one's head above the parapet.

We can see from Schein's work that understanding an organization's culture and where it has come from is not necessarily straightforward. The questions that need to be asked must go deeper: questions about the beliefs which people hold, the assumptions that people make when making a decision, spending a budget or changing team structures. Questions that understand the problem-solving methodology, how solutions are created and who is involved, and what it looks like when the pressure is on. Questions on what behaviour is rewarded and what behaviour is ignored and questions that ask about the perceptions of the internal teams.

Only by really exploring the deeper level of culture – the assumptions, the values displayed – will you then identify whether they are congruent with the artefacts and company values and whether what you have is the culture you want.

Here's an example. I was in a company, researching a merger that had taken place seven years before, and I could tell very quickly that the whole situation was a land mine. The current culture was dire, and in speaking to the employees, it was clear that they were still scarred by the takeover. It was never spoken about as a merger... The words that followed always referred to that time when 'they collided the businesses together'. People were still bruised, and there was still very much an 'us and them' attitude. When I asked why they stayed in a business that had made them so unhappy, it was mostly because they didn't want to leave the part of the business they were in – as they didn't want any more people 'from the other side' getting into their area. It was ludicrous! To me, it was like standing in the queue for a food van when someone offers you dinner at the Savoy, and saying 'no thanks, I don't want to lose my spot!'

To say there wasn't a strong culture would be completely wrong. The culture was *so* strong. Politics were rife; people referred to 'the other side'... and by other side I mean the other physical side of the same building, each naming the other side 'the dark side'. Humanity was gone, and what was left was a whole host of assumptions, made because of how employees were made to feel during the process. Instead of working to build the performance and culture of two organizations, the leaders went in gladiator style, not seeing the long-term damage on those they employed. Years later, still the labels stuck. No effort had gone into understanding who they were and how they could work together effectively. The artefacts said one thing, the company values another – but the basic assumptions were not where they needed to be. Strong culture, yes. Effective? Not by a long shot.

Competing Values Framework

The Competing Values Framework, or CVP, emerged from research to identify organizational culture and organizational dynamics.[2] The framework gives a classification of

---

[2] T. Yu and N. Wu, 'A review of study on the Competing Values Framework'. *International Journal of Business and Management,* 4(7), 37–42 (2009).

four corporate cultures. It is more complex than Schein's three-factor theory. The framework was built off the back of a tonne of research which resulted in the discovery of two major dimensions.

The first dimension relates to **organizational focus**, which ranges from an *internal* focus on wellbeing and development of people in the organization, to an *external* focus on the wellbeing and development of the organization itself.

The second dimension differentiates **organizational preference for structure** and this represents the contrast between *stability and control* and *flexibility and change*.

This is paradoxical, hence the name! The theory has continued to evolve and now in simpler terms the four competing values have been identified as **Collaborate (Clan), Create (Adhocracy), Control (Hierarchy) or Compete (Market).**

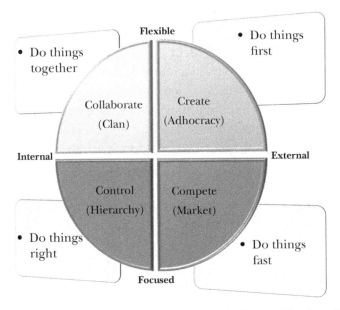

Competing Values Framework, based on Quinn and Rorbaugh[3]

---

[3] R. Quinn and J. Rohrbaugh, 'A spatial model of effectiveness criteria: Toward a Competing Values approach to organizational analysis'. *Management Science*, 29, 363–377 (1983).

Below is a brief description of each of the four competing values; you may find that you can immediately associate some organizations with each of these values.

Collaborate (*Clan culture*)

These organizations typically resemble a large family. A cohesive team with a high level of flexibility. The organization is internally focused – their people, their employees are core to the business. There is a strong sense of loyalty on the part of the business and the employee.

The leadership in the business will be approachable, pull (ask) over push (tell). Leaders who empower their people.

How this might look in the physical environment: teams working cross-functionally, agile teams, open-plan offices, creative and collaborative areas. Making it easy for the employees to work together.

Create (*Adhocracy culture*)

These organizations also operate with a high degree of flexibility, but their focus is external. Dynamic and innovative, creating future solutions for the customer will be at the heart of what they do. They can be seen as the rule breakers.

Leaders often seen as visionaries, and also risk takers. These organizations want their product or service to be the industry leader; therefore, personal initiative will be encouraged. When they fail, they learn from their mistakes.

The physical environment is creative and innovative, with tools designed for their employees to create and thrive.

Control (*Hierarchical culture*)

Hierarchical cultures execute control which is internally focused. Procedures, processes and spans of control are dominating factors. Organized work and clean processes create an environment where the organization runs smoothly and efficiently. The governance of the organizations and the

attention to detail give it stability, and the results relate to efficiency in process.
Leadership along with process is far more bureaucratic; innovation is potentially stifled for the demand of consistent process.
The environments are typically formal and structured.

Compete (*Market culture*)

Opposite to the flexibility of the *Collaborate* and *Create* culture, the *Compete* culture poses a high degree of controlling behaviour. Coupled with the external focus, these are the organizations where speed and results are king.

The employees are actively encouraged to be competitive. Goal oriented, leaders will strive for success and reputation in the external market and manage performance closely to ensure that the goals are achieved. They are fast decision makers with directive traits.

Within the environment, targets, achievements, awards and top performers are all very clearly on display; this is an organization that has an ego and that will be known.

These values compete in a very real sense, and are often determined by resources, leadership, time and budget. For example, if you have identified that you are in the *Control* category and yet your core strategy is to go into new markets (or you have a need to increase your pace of change because you've just been smacked in the face with a global pandemic!) then let's face right up to this. It's not going to be easy, as culturally you have a Ben Nevis to climb.

To complete this assessment on your own organization you can access cultural assessments, such as the Organizational Culture Assessment Instrument (OCAI). This particular assessment consists of a series of questions, made up of the 'as is culture' and questions about the 'to be culture'. The questions are typically put forward to a cross-section of key stakeholders from across the business. You can do this either by sending the report out for individuals to complete alone, or you create forums to debate collectively and to delve deeper into the questions. My preferred method is to do both; participation and involvement is key to cultural development.

The output is a report which identifies the dominant culture, which is the area where the most points are awarded to a particular culture type. The higher the points, the stronger the culture.

This is further broken down into six key elements:

- Dominant characteristics
- Organizational leadership
- Management of employees
- Organization glue
- Strategic emphasis
- Criteria for success

With a clear visual, as a business you will see how close, or how far, you are from your 'target culture', and with the associated breakdown into the six areas, you can then identify which are your priority areas.

The golden thread

These, of course, are just a couple of the theories around organizational culture. There's lots of material out there: Geert Hofstede, Charles Handy, *Harvard Business Review* along with numerous cultural assessment tools. They all have a place: they can all provide the information you need to assess your current culture and uncover your 'target culture'. These sources can provide you with the terminology to make what you're doing sound academic, but ultimately it all comes down to the same thing: diagnose your culture and then focus on what your target culture is, or vice versa; this has to work for you.

The real beauty is that you can do this alone or invite a company in that can facilitate this for you. At Culture Creator we have developed cultural assessments tools personalized to the company's language based on the theories of the greats. Culture is complex, so in my view simplicity needs to be brought to the process to make these digestible and action led. We work with our clients to define which culture will deliver their strategic priorities faster and more effectively. And in a climate where mental health is at its peak, how can your culture create an environment that allows your employees to bring their true self to work each day and feel safe in doing so?

This is the start of the *golden thread*. First, define what you have. Then untangle that thread: align your values with your strategy (the stronger they are the greater the gold). Finally, identify where the thread binds strategy and purpose with your people in a way that holds true. Be authentic: acknowledge where you are and where you want to be, and then take every step to weave consistency of culture through the business and your people.

2

Untangling the thread

The data story of your business

Having addressed the academic theory in Chapter 1, we can now untangle the thread in your own business with information available to you. To do that we will first look at what data you have and what that data tells us; data that indicates your existing culture and data that you may decide to track to measure the effectiveness of your cultural development.

Ongoing data tracking is an essential part of validating cultural alignment; it will show you what's working and what's not, allowing you to then make informed decisions. It might be key to explain here why I don't use the term 'culture change'. Change alludes to there being a start and an end. But where culture is concerned, there is no end! Cultural development is the ongoing nurturing of a conscious culture, and without the ongoing data who's to say the culture you have is the one you set out to achieve?

Using the data gathering template

To support your data gathering, this chapter includes a template where you can capture your findings within your own business. This is an essential part of the book: it will help you interpret what is being said, and equally what is not. Photocopy this template to scribble on, create your own version in a spreadsheet or document, write directly on it or, best still, access our website and receive a free downloadable copy... It doesn't matter which option you choose, but it will really help you get a clear picture on what your information is telling you.

We will look at both external and internal data. Let's have a look at the sections in the template.

External data: Glassdoor rating

What are your employees saying? Look up employee reviews for your company on Glassdoor. Review them – but be subjective, as many organizations are consciously or unconsciously manipulating this data.

'Well done, you've successfully passed your probation... so please can you take a minute and leave a Glassdoor review?' If this kind of sentence sounds familiar, then this is a red flag: if reviews are manipulated and cultivated in this way, what does this tell you about the culture?

Former employees who have taken the time to leave a glowing review after they have left: now *that* has meaning. That suggests a business that understands the full employee journey and has taken active steps to ensure that they have left the door open for that person to return. This reveals something about the culture: that it was created for that purpose.

External data: Trustpilot rating

What are your customers saying? This goes back to the organization's purpose. Is it there to make money or to ensure that the quality of the product or service they offer is impeccable? If they focus on customer service and it's at the heart of their agenda, then you would hope that they have put two and two together and recognized that to achieve excellent customer service, which is delivered by people, then *valued people* can make that happen. Without valuing your people, then the service will be inconsistent. Some will still be great, of course, but some will be average and some absolutely appalling.

External data: Social media

What is the organization's public face? Now this is fascinating, and such an indicator of what the business is about. The PR posts are great, marketing have done an amazing job but the comments – they are switched off. What does that tell you? Are you an open, transparent business? Absolutely not, and the angry-faced emojis stacking up on the left-hand side of the post and the 2,000 comments you can't view is a clear indicator that this is a business that is shying away from what it is truly like to be a customer. If you don't want to listen to the customer, what chance is there that you're listening to your own employees?

Internal data: Employee engagement survey

Traditionally, many big businesses run an annual survey to measure employee engagement – maybe they even have a team whose job it is to do so. But be aware: just like Glassdoor and social media, the analysis could still be manipulated. If you really want to ensure you are getting to the root of the existing culture, then make sure that the data from this has been gathered in its raw form.

Review the questions first, not the answers – and definitely not the engagement score resulting from the survey which the engagement team got to by slicing, dicing and presenting the 'if you squint hard enough' number. The questions asked are informative, as they will show what the organization seems to value the most – but it's the questions that haven't been asked that might be more important.

- Do you believe in the leaders of this business and what they are trying to achieve?
- Do you have everything you need to thrive in your role?
- Do you feel appreciated?
- Do you work as a team towards one purpose?
- Would you recommend xxx as a great place to work?

Do any of these questions appear in the survey? From their appearance – or non-appearance – you will know if the business leadership understands the business vision, and you will understand the leadership qualities that are prevalent, and those that are not. You can see whether or not the culture is one where people are appreciated, rewarded and valued and one where the common goal is a collective effort.

Annual surveys vs. 'pulse' surveys

In recent years, there has been a step change away from the traditional annual survey. Instead, many businesses are choosing to implement pulse surveys: text message or online surveys, which are sent out to a small population, to provide insights to a specific situation, such as a start-up or a key business project. These surveys, rather than being used once a year to try and get the whole picture at once, are used to measure the effectiveness and engagement of a specific part of the business, at specific times. They may be a tool that could be useful for you in your business, but remember this: for a business that wants to *truly* learn – one that genuinely wants to become something great – these pulse surveys will go out whether the project has been a success or a failure.

You can tell what kind of business you are in by looking at how the survey is handled: what questions are asked, what questions aren't, and most importantly, what is done with the output? How honestly has the data been reviewed? How receptive have you been to taking on board the comments and then responding? What have you done with the insights gained from the survey, and how effective do your employees find your surveys? If you have employees saying they are a waste of time, then they are. The surveys should not be for HR, or even for the board: they should be for the employees.

Because they believe what they contribute helps shapes the future of the company.

Once you have considered the questions being asked in the survey, it's time to consider whether you are in a business which listens, or a business that just does the talking. Listening is key to business success. Not just hearing, but truly *listening*. A business with an environment where everyone is taught to listen is a truly magical business. It's one that understands that everyone has something valuable to say – that everyone, every single person, can offer something that we don't already have.

If the business you are in wants to listen and learn, then employee engagement is one of your cultural indicators. But keep asking yourself: are you asking the right questions and truly listening to what your employees are saying? Then, how are you acting on what they are saying?

Employee forums/unions

'Voice of the employee' forums have long been established as an employee engagement tool, but do they truly work? When using your data-gathering template, there are a few things you should be looking for other than the raw output of these forums.

First, establish the purpose of the forums. Are they an opportunity for the employees to share what is working and what is not, or are they a way for the business to circulate an idea or concept for employee feedback? Or both? The purpose and practice of the forums will tell you more about what the culture really is.

Once you have looked at the purpose of any union or forum, look at how it is used in practice. Is there regular attendance? What stops employees from attending? Who is involved in the forum? And possibly the most important factor here: are the employees listened to? Like your surveys, you need to look at what is done with the outcome from any forums or unions or employee focus groups.

A note on unions

Unions will give you the voice of the employee as a collective. However, an employee union should not be the only forum for employees' voices to be heard. Who is speaking to the people 'on the ground' and non-unionized employees? These valuable people often have ideas about the real issues in the business and ideas for continuous improvement; improvement that benefits their working day, which in turn ultimately benefits the business.

People metrics

Later in the book, we will be looking at the full employee lifecycle. For the purposes of this data gathering, however, we need first to look at a range of simple metrics that can be used as indicators about the people in your business. Dependent on the size, scale and sophistication of the business, you may be able to access some, none or all of the following. If you can't access anything, then it may be that HR and available management information need to be challenged. Business decisions are made daily based on people, so doing this without people metrics will only lead to uninformed and potentially bad decisions.

To help define your current culture, you need to gather data on some or all of these things:

- Attrition – a gradual reduction in the number of people who work for an organization that is achieved by not replacing those who leave.
- Turnover – the rate at which employees leave a company and are replaced by new employees (voluntary and involuntary).
- Staff turnover within the first three months of employment.
- Sickness.
- Disciplinaries/grievances/tribunals – are they higher or lower than what you expected?
- Cost and time to hire a new employee.

- Overtime arrangements – who has access to overtime, and what is the total expense of that to the business?
- Diversity measures – think race, gender, age, educational background, socio-economic indicators.
- Average length of service within the business.
- When a new manager starts, how do the metrics change and how is that tracked?
- Who has accountability for these measures and how are their people performance metrics being incorporated into their overall performance within the business?
  - To know whether you have an effective manager, just look at their outputs. If their style is not sustainable with the team, then you immediately know any results will be short-lived. We have all met that manager who seems exceptional to their superiors, as they are smashing out the results; but at what cost? It could be at the cost of team morale due to being overworked and at the cost of the culture you are trying to create.
- What percentage of the total number of people attend training?
- Are your employees given the time to attend the training they need, or does business demand remove them from developing further?
  - Drill down further here and look at the split from a technical learning provision against behavioural development course take-up. Is there a difference? As a business, what is the culture: does it value technical capability over instilling the right behaviours? Are you a business striving to make this a great place to be, or are you driving a culture of performance through your employees' technical capability?
  - Even further still, are your employees being trained in the right skills at the right time? What evidence do you have as a business that shows you are effectively meeting the development needs of your people?
- Any other clearly identifiable trends.
- Add any other data sources you have that will support your understanding of the culture within your business.

The data gathering template

Glassdoor rating ....

Glassdoor comments, please circle your responses below for:

Positive comments:	Authentic	Not authentic
Leavers' comments:	Positive	Negative

Overall thoughts

....

....

....

....

Trustpilot rating ....

What are the customers saying   Positive   Negative

....

....

....

....

Social media ....

Capture what you have learnt ....

....

Employee engagement survey .... Overall engagement score

Population completed .... Frequency ....

How many questions? ....

Could they be reduced?	Yes	No
Action plans in place?	Yes	No

Commentary – Key learnings ....

....

....

....

....

Established and effective employee forums?	Yes	No
Established and effective union relationship	Yes	No

People metrics

You may wish to review the last 12 months of data. As this is your baseline, take the average, then you can measure impact each month against the baseline.

Attrition ....

Turnover ....

Staff turnover within first three months ....

Disciplinary ....

Grievances .... Tribunal ....

Sickness ....

Cost per hire ....

Time to hire ....

Overtime % ....

Diversity measures ....

....

....

....

....

Average length of service ....

Management methods of tracking ....

Average % course fill ....

Technical / behavioural split ....

Development at point of need ....

....

....

....

....

Any identifiable trends? ....

....

Any other data you have found that supports your understanding of your culture ....

Making sense of the data

Now you have completed your internal data-gathering exercise, we can explore what this is telling us in each section:

External perception: How does the external world perceive your business? Are the practices you have around social media and serving your customer indicative of the culture you aspire to have? Are you positioned as a great company that attracts quality people for that reason, or is there work to be done? Ask yourself: 'Does our external story align with our internal culture?' If there is a disconnect, it may result in attracting the wrong candidate, a candidate who is not culturally aligned; it may reduce the talent pool that you are trying to attract from; or if there is a great culture but poor external perception your employees may become fatigued defending a company they love.

Behaviours and practice: The engagement survey will provide you with far greater details regarding key categories, such as how well the strategy is known, how effective the leadership is, to whether the environment is right or not. But along with the content of the survey, what did the practice of it look like? How effective are the processes, from capturing the data through to the completion rates of the surveys, through to the outcomes? Are the calls to action the ones being asked for? Ask yourself: 'Are we invested in listening to our employees and are we taking real action?'

Hard facts: With this data, benchmarking against industry standards will indicate as a business how aligned you are. Being close to the average is acceptable but going below each data category has a financial impact. If you have high turnover in the first three months, explore why. Is it a misaligned narrative, are you selling a dream, which in reality it's not? Or is it down to poor onboarding and management? Cost how much it is to recruit. How much is the impact costing your business? Time to hire also relates to external perception. Are you a business where people are queuing to get in, or are they queuing to get out?

The data and the exploration of it will provide you with themes to look at, areas that you might want to delve into further. Involve your people: make sense of the data, ask if the data is what they expected or whether there is room for improvement. And if there is room for improvement, what does that look like? Ownership will be the catalyst for change.

The data we have looked at is the obvious data with your business; couple this with the cultural assessment and you will now have the outline of the 'as is' and the start of defining your 'to be' target culture. You might also decide at this point whether the data you have just captured you want to track monthly to show your cultural progression. If there is data that has alarmed you, or you want to see a shift, then track it. Attribute a cost to it and see how shaping the culture can impact that cost.

If your target culture is to drive faster innovation to market, then capture the statistics that will evidence this; identify how you are going to track these on an ongoing basis. Do you have a team who can do this for you, or is this a data-gathering exercise that's manual at present but for the sake of longevity needs to become automated? What do you need to do to make that happen?

Those measures become your cultural tracking tool, which you can use throughout the year to measure the alignment of the culture against your target culture. What would the measures/indicators need to be for your culture to be fulfilled? Start with the end in mind and measure on a monthly basis, and of course if you have used a cultural assessment tool, then repeat it in 6/12/18/24 months' time. What is it telling you now?

Culture has a commercial impact: what does your data inform you about the cost impact? Forecast the savings based on the cultural shift that you want to see and track it. It will show you the commercial value to the business of why you are doing this, along with the benefits for the employees.

It may be that you are in a smaller organization where you're thinking the above sounds great in practice, but not in reality. But the time and effort you can put into this will be well served. As you have identified the data available to you, look at how you can capture it monthly, even if this a manual process. Set up a management meeting with those who need to be there and look at the data. Interpret it together, identify the triggers, what has changed to make an impact, what needs to be explored further, what is the data telling you? Over time, you will evolve this, different data will be gathered, a spreadsheet created, and some whizz will have created you the dashboard you need.

However you choose to capture this data, this is your story, one that's easier to articulate and use to gain buy-in. You can use it to achieve clarity over where you are and where you're headed. Your teams then have a choice: they can choose to listen and take action or they can choose to ignore it. Either way, you have transparency and then you have choice. How serious you are about your culture will depend on how serious you are about taking action to correct what doesn't align with it.

3

The thread of thought

Creating a culture

Start with the goal in mind: Presenting your target culture

If you have used a cultural assessment tool that questions both the 'as is' and the 'to be' culture, you will have started to form what you want your target culture to be. It may include behaviours; it may face up to processes that need to be changed, environmental impact or even how the organizational structures might need to change. However, before moving onto the detail of target culture design, we will consider the design of the future culture you want to share with your employees. This involves selecting the communication tool you will ultimately use to gain buy-in and engagement around how you see your future business.

Starting with the end in mind, decide what the purpose of the communication tool for your target culture will be and then on the best format. As this is typically designed for all employees, the information given by the communication tool is likely to focus on organizational behaviours.

You may decide you don't want anything to go to your employees, and the document you design will be a tool for the leaders only. It could be that the design is your communication tool that you want printed out and placed around your buildings, or to go one step further to roll out the culture to all employees. The output tool will be used for training. How you want to roll this out will need to be decided upfront.

Here are a few variations to help your thinking:

- Culture board
- Culture statement
  - ○ Code of conduct
  - ○ Customer impact statement
- Cultural wheel
- Competency framework

We will look at each of these formats in more detail below – but first, let's look at how to decide on a tool in a way that will work for your business and go forward with maximum buy-in.

Culture on a page (defining your aspiration)

The first step in the design process is to create a one-page document based on what your culture will be. Keep it short and succinct.

This document typically includes:

- Why is this culture important to us?
- A culture statement which outlines your target culture, which can then be broken further down into cultural indicators – how you will be able to see and tell that the target culture is in place.

The best way to capture this is through a facilitated session. Hold a focus session with the leadership, knowing that this one-pager will be the key output. The one-pager should be designed to capture all the points and your role is to validate through active challenge. What is captured will then have real commitment from leaders and participants.

Your document could also include how you will assess against the indicators, what measures are in place and why it is important – don't forget, this is an ongoing process. It may even include targets; if you have a particularly clear agenda of what you want and when you want it, then shout about it.

Lastly, you may choose to include the question of *what happens when?* What happens when people don't act in accordance with the culture you are trying to create? Don't be afraid of this question: you're either in it or you're not. How do people hold each other to account? How do they hold the leadership team to account? What licence are you giving people to stay true to the culture and how are you equipping them to challenge misalignment?

Cultural alignment isn't easy; it can be very difficult, especially if there are ingrained behaviours. If you are committed to the change in culture, then consider the following: How are you going to allow people to feel safe when raising challenges and to feel protected in doing so?

These are the questions you need to consider upfront. Do not wait until you are rolling out some fancy framework. Make sure the questions, the difficult questions, are asked at the very beginning. If the leaders are not in agreement this will be difficult to follow through.

Now let's take a closer look at some of the formats, or expressions, your new culture might take.

Culture statement

As with any statement, this is a great exercise to truly hone what everyone around the table wants the culture to be, and what they can agree on. The statement should be thought out and carefully considered. If this is going to be shared with your employees then it also needs to be engaging; it needs the employee to *get* it, to understand what is acceptable and what's not. Engaging makes it real; dry makes it forgettable.

There are a few variations of what a culture statement can include. You might want to consider entwining one or more of these features:

Impact statement: Something that explains the impact of non-culturally aligned behaviour.

Code of conduct: I have seen culture statements entwined with an organization's 'code of conduct'. Slightly more in depth than a simple impact statement, this is a statement that typically talks about both acceptable and unacceptable conduct.

A word of caution on this. If you're going to produce a code of conduct for your employees, don't make it 50 pages long; this should not be a legal get-out covering all eventualities document – don't pop it in their contract pack asking for a signed copy back and that's it. This would be tenuous, shows that little investment and time are put into what's acceptable, and the behaviours will be as weak lived as the effort put into it.

For this to work, you have to make it *real*. Make it short and sharp, and check understanding from the employees' side. Make sure it is owned, and that the owners are going back and checking that the code is still correct for the business and really lends itself to the culture the organization is trying to achieve. If not, then dust it off, challenge it. Does it ring true? Does it bring the beliefs of the business alive? Does it make you truly understand the type of business you're in? If not – change it. In all honesty, I have very mixed feelings about codes of conduct. It may be that they are needed in some organizations – maybe it really is the right approach for your company? But if you don't need it, then be creative; think outside of the box!

Customer impact statement: In businesses that do the culture statement well already, there will often be something similar for the customers, so customers know what type of organization you are, they know how they will be treated, and what they should expect. It's transparent and contact with the organization is seamless because of it. This will also be clearly understood by the employees; with a customer impact statement, they will know exactly how to treat their customers and they know the type of organization they are in. Whatever variation you use, when developed effectively, the culture statement is short, sharp and succinct, and becomes easy to communicate. It has *impact*: it says what it is on the tin. It's your elevator pitch for your business, and when it's real it's the thread that binds everyone to the strategy and purpose.

Cultural wheel

Another way in which organizations are presenting their culture is with the creation of a 'cultural wheel'. This is a more visual way of presenting the culture statement along with behaviours and values to represent the company culture. Personally, I love a visual, and I have seen these to be really effective! To keep it impactful, keep it clean; don't over engineer it. Importantly, too: don't make this a fad. Don't play 'Wheel of Fortune' with it! Unless you have already adopted this gameshow-style culture – and not many brands will authentically adopt this cultural style – it will simply look like a gimmick. You've just turned something that was supposed to have depth and meaning into a game and as much as we'd all have a go at spinning the wheel, the takeaway would be the prize and not the true purpose of what you are trying to achieve.

The cultural wheel is a great example of where you need to have asked: 'What is the purpose of its design?' If the purpose is a tool to train and engage your employees, then this is a great way to go. The wheel can be developed as a floormat: your training out of the target culture can then be physical with your teams walking through each component. By bringing the future to life in physical form, your teams can walk through the behaviours, they can absorb themselves in the rationale and it will leave an impression. And that's what you are after: creating a tool that helps people thread together the new culture will pay dividends in the adoption process.

Competency framework

You may decide to take a more detailed approach to showcasing your culture (particularly in control cultures), and that might be in the form of a competency framework. This describes the skills, attributes and knowledge required for a role within the business – a little bit like a person specification or a job description that you may be familiar with from recruiting. In fact, with a clear and defined competency framework, you can indeed use them to recruit – and to manage performance. Competency frameworks have been around for a while, and in some workplaces they may be considered a bit 'old hat'; but in others, they are recently becoming more prominent.

The introduction of the apprenticeship levy in the UK in 2017, along with the new *standards*, means that industries have seen and will continue to see this style of document. The new *standards* consist of knowledge, skills and behaviours. Where industries have a high number of apprentices this type of documentation is the norm. The *standards* meet the needs of the employer while ensuring the learner gets the full suite of desired learning outcomes. Also, in any business where there are institutes or governing bodies, a competency framework is expected.

The positives of this approach are that leaders have a crystal-clear guide to follow. Each role has the competencies mapped out, both behavioural and technical. The behavioural competencies can be aligned to the values, but then key competencies are dependent on the role. New starters are assessed against them, and it is easy to make sure fairness is applied. Existing employees are performance measured against them. Clear indicators show what they need to be doing to reach the next level. It's transparent, it's detailed, and it makes for an easy conversation, as any feedback is fact based. Using pre-defined expectations as a measure, there is little room or need for subjectivity. Development can be easily curated in line with the needs of the competencies – so it's far easier for the employee to own their own development. If you have decided that as a business you require that level of detail, then a competency framework lends itself perfectly towards the culture you are trying to curate. It provides the detail, the narrative, it sets expectations, and it shows fairness.

Of course, there are downsides, too: the main one being the sheer volume of detail. To really assess someone against the framework properly, you would need to have the document in your hand. It can then feel like more of a personal audit, or a formal assessment, than a fluid one-to-one conversation. It can be a little dogmatic for some; working through a framework with your manager in a one-to-one meeting risks sacrificing the value of real, genuine conversation, and leaves little opportunity to get under the skin of your employee. Nor will this document cover the wider cultural impact, process, environmental changes, structural changes and so on.

Frameworks *can* be made cool and contemporary, but the art in designing them comes with knowing what their purpose is and having the buy-in from those who will use them. As with anything you communicate, your teams need to understand the 'why'. Design the frameworks with the people who are going to use them, trial them, make them detailed enough to meet these needs... but don't destroy the quality of the conversation. Create them in a way that allows the employee to self-audit – you could create an app, send round a few questions a day which are linked to the competencies, and make the process slick, not paper laden. Take a traditional format and make it effective for you.

Define and refine your purpose for its design. The framework is only of any value when the culture is presented so that it can be understood by all. Design it to be as future proof as you can make it. This will be the tool that all new starters will need to be educated with and that all existing employees will adopt.

The format in which you decide to present your target culture is just the start; it's the blueprint to build from. It's now time to label the areas that your culture addresses in a language which meets the needs of your business.

Many of the cultural assessment tools will provide you with the labels but their generic nature means the language can sometimes be a shade too formal, which can immediately disconnect your audience.

To create a cultural development plan and the associated 'culture design', use authentic and simple language. I use what we call a 'culture board' with my clients.

Culture board

This is my preferred method. Within a culture design session, we work together to create a *culture board*. This is a tool I use to help clients consider the data outputs, the target culture and to then delve into the critical operational and psychological areas of the business to capture in one place. Essentially, is the business built in a way for the target culture to be achieved?

It would typically include:

- **Purpose:** The organizational purpose.
- **Priorities:** So that you focus on the long-term strategic goals of the business.
- **Values:** Here you validate and test the values the business has; are they the ones it needs? (Chapter 4 provides further guidance.)
- **Behaviours:** What do you reward, formally and informally, and what do you turn a blind eye to? Individual and team working behaviours.

- **Processes:** Are the processes in place those that support the target culture? For example, if you are currently a control culture and you want to move to a compete culture, is there red tape that needs removing?
- **Structures:** Organizationally, is your people structure built in a way that supports the desired culture?
- **The narrative:** Does the business story align with the target culture (internal and external)?

Facilitate these questions with the board and your senior leaders. Look at the data you have gathered and determine how close or far you are from your future culture.

As you move into your planning stage, be clear on what it is within each area that you may need to tackle. Culture is input; engagement is output. Culture touches every part of the organization and congruence is about what it should be. How the organization is built is fundamental to progression.

We have an outline; now we need to create the plan.

Time to plan: It's evolution not revolution

It's wise to remember that changing a culture will not happen overnight. Shaping a culture that is authentic to the business and aligned with its purpose and strategy takes time. Know this, but don't hold back: be bold in your culture design and culture statement, be transparent about where you are and where you want to be. Instil in your people that you are after perseverance, not perfection. That when you are working towards something, personally, professionally and organizationally, you demonstrate continued growth. Doing this in a way that is connected means you grow collectively and organizationally more quickly; it provides unity, removes ambiguity and removes the ego. Taking the step to develop a culture may result in some leaders feeling uncomfortable, particularly if the new target culture has significantly different behaviours to their strengths. Being open about what you are trying to achieve, and showcasing the support and development you will be offering, gives licence for leaders to be vulnerable, to make a choice and to hopefully move to a transformational phase. Command and conquer is sidelined for the new leader. They understand that to grow, they must continually develop themselves and others.

Once all of your activity has been captured, then identify how you can truly land this in your business. What will need to happen for the engagement and acceptance to be mobilized? What resources or support will you require? What budget will you need? And then plan your budget accordingly. In your data-gathering exercise, you may have started peeling the layers back on spiralling costs, so what costs are you looking to save, what are your engagement targets and then along with an engaged workforce what could the potential impact be on your business performance?

To recap on our cultural planning, we have:

Defined: We have defined where we are and where we want to be – gap analysis complete. I would also include values and associated behaviour analysis here. That way we are starting with a solid picture and know what foundations we have or don't have in place (see Chapter 4 for more on values).

Aim: Culture needs to be aligned to the strategic priorities – what are they, does the target culture deliver what you need to achieve (the culture board)? Then look at the targets you want to achieve (culture on a page and data-gathering exercise). By defining these in measurable ways, you know exactly what you are aiming for and how you can track the measurements.

Strive: This is the series of prioritized steps that will need to take place to achieve your goal; ongoing management of these will maintain momentum.

Strive will be the formulated plan you will produce, either by using the book or with the support of an associate. This is your action plan aligned with your priorities. You know your business and what you are trying to achieve. But as form of guidance, make sure you cover the following:

- **Communication and engagement strategy:** Explain the 'why' to *all* your employees. Be clear on what you want to achieve and what you expect. Build the story, the narrative of your culture, your business and then deliver it in a compelling way.
- **Implementation activities:** What organizational development needs to take place, what processes reviewed? Do you have policies that no longer fit with your ethos?
- **Artefacts:** Facilities, the environment, what needs to change? Is the environment reflective of the one that will get the most success?
- **Values and behaviours:** If you are changing these, how will you engage and mobilize change? How entrenched the behaviours are will be reflected in the time and effort required to ensure they are changed in the right way.
- **Training and development:** What needs to happen now and in the long term? How do you future-proof the same experience for every new employee joining the business?

This is where you build the plan right for you, challenge yourself on your purpose, choose the culture you want to have, shape it and then look at how through each stage you can see what needs to happen to reinforce who you want to become.

4

Laced in gold

Discovering and defining values

One of the areas that will emerge from the culture board is alignment of organizational values. We need to make the distinction between values and culture a bit clearer.

Values are the foundation. They are fixed and should remain the same throughout everything: they provide a guided framework to how decisions should be made. Culture, on the other hand, will continually evolve – different departments will undoubtedly have variations on the overall company culture. This is because culture, although built on shared values, is shaped by people, leaders and strong influencers. The key to creating a healthy and authentic culture for your business is knowing what your target culture is and being able to weave the golden thread through each and every interaction. This is what drives consistency of behaviour.

This chapter will look solely at values, and the purpose of values. Does your business have them? Do your employees know them or, better still, believe in them?

Values and their purpose in organizations have been questioned and debated considerably: 'Do they have any real worth?' 'Are they just a campaign with no soul?' Or worse: 'They are great, but they contradict the behaviour of the business.' I for one believe that values are a must, but *only* when they are created with the sincerity and dedication they deserve.

Let's first look at our own personal values. If I asked you what they were, could you answer? Or would you need time to reflect? Even with the time to reflect, can you condense your considerations into a handful of true values?

I've raised this point because we all have values – consciously or subconsciously – but every now and then you see them play out; you recognize them and how they have shaped you as an individual. In most large organizations, defining values is a widely prevalent practice. For many, though, some 'values' never truly land, so they change the defined values, they design a new set... and yet again they don't land. When designed unauthentically and not aligned to the overarching purpose and behaviours of the business, then the values are not true values; they are simply a fad. The defined values need to be part of the fabric of the organization. They need to be created so that, along with purpose and mission, they become the tapestry that all employees understand and see acted out.

Not all organizations have defined values, but the following needs to be considered: an organization without values is like a house without foundations. You can have your strategy and goals but misaligned values will make them harder to achieve.

In schools, children are educated in what their school values are. Many schools have nailed this approach: teach, reteach, communicate, recommunicate, and educate the parents. They understand that the right values are the foundation of how everyone – parents, teachers, students – are all expected to behave. And when a student falls out of sync with one of the values, the school can have a straightforward conversation with them to address it and reset expectations.

With millennials and Generation Y already comprising 50% of your workplace, expected to rise to 75% by 2025, they expect values. They have seen them in practice, and they understand the concept. So, if your values are tepid, inauthentic or undefined... you have a generation monopoly who not only will be seeking out the values, but will be trying to understand the conflicts and questioning why everyone is pulling in different directions.

This chapter allows you to reflect on your values as a business and to determine if they are working for you – and if not, *why* not? For those who haven't got organizational values, then we will explore why they will be of value on your journey to cultural hedonism and provide you with the tools to reflect on, gather and then design your own.

Defining values

To effectively complete the next exercise, you will need to have considered both your organizational and personal values.

Organizational values

First, identify within your own business whether you have 'organizational values'.

If you don't, is there a clear rationale for this? Are values something you want to develop? If so, the section on 'Businesses with no values' will explore this further and a section has also been included later in this chapter for those that wish to design new values.

If you do, how easy were they to recall? Did you know them off the top of your head or did you need to look them up?

Personal values

Next, let's look at personal values. Below is a list of value words. Circle those that feel applicable to you and add your own if they are not here; this is not an exhaustive list. Take around ten minutes to complete this task, as it is worth challenging yourself to get your list down to your top four or five chosen personal values.

Ambition, Autonomy, Bravery, Capability, Collaboration, Communication, Decision Making, Devotion, Dignity, Empathy, Equality, Excellence, Family, Feedback, Focus, Frankness, Healthy Challenge, Humility, Humour, Integrity, Kindness, Logic, Mastery, Modesty, Open Mindedness, Passion, Perceptiveness, Perfection, Proactive, Professionalism, Speed, Strength, Realism, Reliability, Resilience, Resourcefulness, Respect, Self-Discipline, Skill, Support, Trust, Vision, Zeal.

....
....
....
....

Now you have yours, do they match the organization you are in?

                                              Yes   No

In your organization, were the values easy to find/get hold of?

                                              Yes   No

Have they properly landed in the business? Essentially, are the values true? Are they used in the organization? If they are used, how are they used? Are the values used to validate business decisions? And ultimately the biggest question: 'When the business is under pressure, what happens to the values?'

                                       Yes   No
                                   Maintained   Forgotten

Added interest: Glassdoor have compiled what they call the 'Big 9 Cultural Values'.[1] These are the values that are most used by the leading companies and have the greatest results.

- Agility
- Collaboration
- Customer
- Diversity
- Execution
- Innovation
- Integrity
- Performance
- Respect

How did the above resonate with your own values and the ones of the business you are in? Are you confident that your values are the right ones and that they resonate with your target culture?

Businesses with 'no values'

If the organization 'has no values', what does that mean? For small organizations where the leader's span of control and influence can touch every employee, then chances are the values are there. There are values prevalent in the decisions being made, the actions being taken, and the conversations taking place... they're just not in written form. But when the organization grows, how does the leader grow their sphere of influence? How do they continue to grow the behaviours

---

[1] E. H. Meyer, 'What aspects of company culture matter most in today's job economy'. Glassdoor for Employers, 6 November 2019. Available from: www.glassdoor.com/employers/blog/what-aspects-of-company-culture-matter-most-in-todays-job-economy [accessed 8 January 2021].

into the business that they want to see? If ethical behaviour is a value, or 'people over profit', for example, then it is clear that embedding these values through business growth will be integral to maintaining the company ethos.

If the ethos and values of the business haven't been shared, then new leaders recruited will make decisions based on what they think is right. Past experiences of a previous organization will likely dominate, and the organization's values could be compromised.

For values to work, there needs to be full alignment across all leaders and expectations. They need to be intrinsically linked to the purpose of the business. Having a shared purpose with aligned values ensures everyone is looking to achieve the same goal in the same way. It means that when you are *not* in the room and part of the decision-making process, you can rely on the fact that the team who are in the room are working with the company values at the forefront of their mind. That way, you know your business is growing and developing but its soul is maintained. It's your defined DNA, your genetic code which is individual to you as a business. This is what sets you apart; it's not the product or service, as these can be replicated. It's the culture, the DNA of your people, that will set you apart.

Businesses with existing 'values'

Time should be dedicated to values design. Values should have been created with purpose and intent. They are so much more than wallpaper for your funky offices; if you're looking for something decorative then make sure your facilities manager or responsible person is familiar with current up-to-date modern design. The 'Old Grey Box' building with grey desks, grey cabinets, grey kit… well, they're grey, and possibly not the most creative of spaces, so don't try and spruce them up with a set of values just for that reason. That is not to say you shouldn't emblazon your values on the wall. If they are the soul of the business and they resonate then absolutely have them around as a soft reminder, but wallpaper does not constitute a communication plan... it's not enough.

If your business has stated values already, let's go back to how the values were created. What was the intention in how they would be used? Let's look at the reality of how effectively they have landed, and how they are applied. Have they been adopted in line with the purpose they were set out to achieve? Are your existing values known and acted out?

To find the answers to the above questions, talk to the employees; consider asking the following:

- Can you give me three words to describe the behaviour of the business?
- Do the values work well?
- Are the values authentic and played out throughout the business?
- What value resonates with you the most (and why)?
- What value resonates with you the least (and why)?
- Are the values easy to recall?
- What is your interpretation of them? (Seek clarity to see if their understanding aligns with the original intent.)
- Do your values have guiding principles?

By obtaining a cross-section of opinions you will soon uncover whether the values are understood, and interpreted, in the same way, or whether the values, albeit easy to recall, are so broad brush that their level of ambiguity has resulted in employees using the values in a way that suits the time and situation. Interpretation, the reason for so many tribunals.

You may discover that through your questioning your employees deem the values as great; everyone loved them; they fully understood the intent and purpose behind each one, and their interpretation was on point. It was just that they had never seen them before, or if they had, it was within an appraisal document they had seen once, 11 months earlier!

Your questioning will help you understand who sees the ongoing embedding of values into the business as their role. Values shouldn't be the responsibility of HR; they should be the responsibility of the business. The responsibility of every employee. If you have a value of 'Integrity', and an employee behaves in an unethical manner, do your employees feel safe to address this?

Do your leaders and managers know the values? Are they well versed in what the values are? Do they give people licence to hold each other to account in line with the defined value? And do they see 'embedding values' as part of their role?

If you have cracked it, and you have values that work for you and your employees; if you are a business that consistently and predictably makes decisions that are aligned to your values, that are aligned to your long-term goals as a business, then you are a VDC, a Values-Driven Company. VDCs are, in their own right, some of the most successful companies. They are renowned for their alignment of people and purpose and shaped with guiding principles that provide employees with a framework for collective success.

If you don't have any values within the business or the values you have aren't authentic to your business and you want to go through a process of introducing or designing new values, then read on.

Designing new values

Step 1: What does this mean to you?

When designing any values, the board needs to be challenged on the following questions. Again, this is not an exhaustive list, so feel free to add your own.

You can run this as a collective session, or you can meet individually. Meeting individually will give you individual insights, which may be very valuable, but be aware that you will have to follow up as a group as well to get collective consensus. Consider asking:

- Why are we creating values; what will their purpose be?
- How will the values be used?
- What is the investment in making sure everyone understands the values?
- What will success look like, of fully understood and executed values?
- What is your level of commitment here and what does commitment mean to you?
- How do the values map to the vision, mission and purpose of the business?
- Without them, what could the impact be?

You should now have an understanding at board level of what this means. Is there real commitment? Values need to be business-led, not HR-led. This is not an initiative; this is the board growing its sphere of influence in alignment with the growth of the business. This is the business delivering on its objectives, to achieve its vision, with all its employees working towards them in the desired manner.

What do values truly mean to the board? What are they willing to forego for the ethics and behaviours within their business to be acceptable – for example, are they willing to sacrifice a certain level of profit or a lucrative contract to ensure the company is working ethically? Are they committed to being challenged on their own decision making and behaviours, in line with the defined values? To be willing to be held to account is where you want them to be. To be accepting of challenge. To be willing for someone to hold up the mirror to them when times are good... but more importantly when times are bad. And most importantly, not only willing for the mirror to be held up to them – but for the person who is holding up the mirror to feel safe in doing so.

If you have just gone through the above process and the commitment is not there, you need to get to the bottom of where the resistance is coming from. You need to spend time listening and asking incisive questions. Be prepared: have these questions mapped out when you are going into your session. This is where you need to facilitate the room in a way that asks for a contribution from each person. Go in prepared with printed questions so that should you be met with resistance, you call a halt, hand out the questions and state that you want to understand more from each of them. Take ten minutes to complete them individually. This is a great method of really finding out who thinks what; where is the negativity coming from? Or who is it coming from? And if you have only been given a 20-minute slot with the board on values, then this is as achievable as trying to milk a cow with oven gloves on. Slightly achievable but not a particularly comfortable experience on any side and a clear indicator of the culture. So my advice would be engage, ask the questions, and follow up with the uncomfortable ones.

- Why does this not work for you?
- Do you understand your impact as a board? (If you don't believe in it, no one else will!)
- What's stopping you from buying into values working?
- What would this business look like if values resonated with everyone?
- What would it look like if we had no values?

Ask questions that remove assumptions. We all have paradigms; a way in which we view the world. You may have leaders who have seen values not work. There may be little trust in the department they believe this belongs to. Either way, your role is to realign with the board that culture is simply 'the way we do things around here'.

Failing that, ask the board what they think the cost is of a good versus a poor culture. Have your numbers ready. You captured your data already, you have the commercial understanding and you have forecasted the cost savings of a potential cultural shift. This is your chance to show that the commercial impact is *real*, high turnover has a cost, absence has a cost, retraining has a cost, disciplinaries, management time, loss of customers, brand damage... they all have a cost and they will all be impacted. Articulate the cost in a way that identifies the culture with the current business challenges.

I can't promise this will be easy, of course – but it's a process that needs to be explored. It may make you ultimately realize that what is being tasked may be of no gain. You may have a lightbulb moment. Is this the place where you want to be, or do you think you have the commitment that the board will drive this through? You may be a board member and you understand what the challenges ahead are and who within the leadership team is aligned culturally with the values you have and who is not. But get this right and you'll be working with an engaged business full of people who all know their roles, why they are here and how they should be achieving the business goal.

Step 2: Let's get defining

Next, you can start identifying what the values of the business should be. Or, if they are already in existence: are they known, have they landed and are they true?

There are many ways to do this, internally led or with the assistance of an external supplier or consultant. If you decide to handle it internally, you could try an exercise using 'value cards', or even a company survey.

Value cards and forums

Hold forums and get participating employees to identify what the active business values are. Provide cards with value words on them, and ask participants to select the cards that they identify most with, on behalf of their role in the business.

Write up the words on a flipchart or whiteboard to identify the consistencies – which words keep being selected? It's important to keep reinforcing that these are the values of the *business* and not personal values; personal values can easily overshadow the purpose of the activity if you let them. It may also be worthwhile having the company's vision, mission and purpose up on the wall or otherwise readily available for this activity.

Values survey

Issue a survey to gather data. Ask employees what they think are the values that are demonstrated in the business, and equally what are not. The latter always produces some interesting results.

Complete it with multiple groups, with wide demographics of the working population. Alternatively, you could complete it with the board, if they want to agree the aspirational or future values of the business rather than what they currently actually are. The beauty of doing both, of course, is that it will then provide you with a benchmark; it will tell you how far from or close you are to having the business operate in the same conducive way. From your findings, you can build your plan on how you will close that gap. It's also a great indicator for how close your board are to being aware of the real culture in the business.

Test and refine

Whatever method you use, refine the data you gather until you have really *nailed* the values. Be prepared to counter-argue each one. Go back to the leaders of the business, and place scenarios in front of them; realistic scenarios that will challenge the values. Ensure everyone is truly in agreement and you can be assured you have got the values right, and that they are more than just a collection of words. This is especially important if the leaders select values without drawing any insights from employees and the wider business: in this case, test them further, throw scenarios at them that will challenge their thinking, counter-argue, stress test them, do everything you can to check that the board truly believe in the values they have selected – do this, and they will stick.

Step 3: Let's get creative

Once you have decided on your values – and remember, that will take time and refinement – then decide how you want them presented. Presentation is key to ensuring your values land effectively. You may recall a LinkedIn post that went viral in 2019, featuring the company Huel who had an office wall printed with their opening statement, 'Don't be a dick.'[2] This is blunt, it is memorable – but is it effective? We have to be mindful of the type of business it is, and the employees and clients it attracts. Suitability and effectiveness can only be based on really *knowing* your audience (and not from whether a concept goes viral online).

We are in an evolving society. What was once unacceptable is now seen as cool and contemporary. If you are a new and vibrant organization, your values and their design need to reflect this. If you have been in business for years, however, and your organization is built on family traditions… then stay true to those traditions and don't try to be something you're not. Authenticity will help you to embed the new values effectively.

Defining values can be tricky, but pulling the final value words together in a way that feels like one authentic, cohesive whole that can be shared and remembered is even trickier – especially for a large organization. Many businesses go down the mnemonic route, which is brilliant when it works,

---

[2] Huel, LinkedIn post, 2019. Available from www.linkedin.com/posts/huel_1-year-at-huel-hq-activity-6630425261647233024-bcez [accessed 18 January 2021].

but when it doesn't... *wow* you can tell! There will be one value that really doesn't resonate, but we needed a value that started with a *T*... so *tenacity* it is! Whichever style you use – just four to five words, mantras, a mnemonic, or even lengthy statements – knowing the business style, the purpose and how the values will be used will support you in ensuring that the creative guidelines are correct. Of course, you can go maverick and wacky, and this will certainly grab attention... but will people really buy into them? Take into consideration that flair can be attractive, but style over substance will be detrimental.

There are some amazing agencies that can help with this, but for now, let's look at a couple of examples.

Adidas: Statement-type values

Some organizations go for statement-type values. Adidas are a great example of this. Their group values are elaborated in fuller, sentence-style explanations (*guiding principles*), but as simple words can be remembered as Performance, Passion, Integrity and Diversity. Neat – memorable, even – and with a solid and clear explanation validating exactly what each value stands for. It's nice; it paints the picture of a company that knows who they are. From this, we can tell that they have integrity, and that they will maintain that integrity for the sake of their brand. You know where you stand with Adidas.

Adidas

Performance – Sport is the foundation for all we do and executional excellence is a core value of our group.

Passion – Passion is at the heart of our company. We are continuously moving forward, innovating and improving.

Integrity – We are honest, open, ethical and fair. People trust us to adhere to our word.

Diversity – We know it takes people with different ideas, strengths, interests and cultural backgrounds to make our company succeed. We encourage healthy debate and differences of opinion.[3]

Build-A-Bear: Cutesy

Then there are those that go full-on cutesville. Build-A-Bear, the children's personalized soft-toy company, have come up with an ingenious list of utterly cute values. This approach can go really, really wrong if you're not careful – let's face it, cutesy is not going to be the right approach for many serious brands – but you would *have* to be cute to be a successful part of the Build-A-Bear team! Despite my personal feelings about the level of cute required to stay sane in a world of unicorn-vomit, I do fully admire those who can be child entertainers for a full shift, dealing with hundreds of children and exasperated parents. So, my anti-unicorn feelings aside... what Build-A-Bear did was clever. They get 10/10 from me for creativity – the values below appealed to their employees, it was good-natured and it was honest fun. Ultimately, their value words are aligned to the business – and despite how many there are, I have never experienced anything but those values when parting with my money (which is typically, an inordinate amount) in the cutesville stores!

Build-A-Bear

Reach
Learn
Di-bear-sity

---

[3] Adidas Group, 'Vision and values'. Available from https://bit.ly/3pYeX64 [accessed 8 January 2021].

Colla-bear-ate
Give
Cele-bear-ate[4]

Whatever approach you take, remember that it's important not to be bulldozed by one person's point of view. Your values have to have wider consensus to ensure they are endorsed and upheld throughout the company. The values and culture need to be congruent, so make sure the values don't contradict what you are trying to achieve. Time well spent on this step will ensure you have the right values. This is where you have started to lay the foundations, and with solid foundations you can then start looking at how you build the house.

Business values designed, it's time to regroup. Get your target audience together and identify what works for them, what doesn't work. Test out the values and after some final editing, agree on the design that you will take forward.

Congratulations – this is a monumental moment! You now have a series of values that are interwoven into the purpose, the vision and the mission of the business – and they are *real*. You have stress tested them, and they held their value (excuse the pun!).

Position and planning

You are now moving into the realms of purpose, position and planning. Having already explored the purpose of the values and how they will be used, let's now identify where the values will be incorporated and ensure that this purpose is still aligned.

---

[4] These are the original Build-A-Bear values that have since changed; for the up-to-date values, see www.buildabear.com/brand-about-careers-working-here.html [accessed 18 January 2021].

Consider how your values are going to affect:

- Competencies – leader and employee
- Interview questions
- Onboarding documentation and experience
- Communications
- People development programmes
- Reward and recognition

By no means is this list exhaustive, and as you move into Chapter 5 you will uncover more thinking around how you want your values and culture to be shaped. Each thread of the employee lifecycle shows you that through applying layer after layer of continuity you are lacing together the values and culture to all your employees.

Here are a couple of examples of the thinking that you will need to walk through to achieve this.

Recruitment and selection

If you recruit against values or have competencies built under each value, how effective is this? Is your recruitment process working and how are you measuring the quality of the person you hire? It is incredibly powerful to have aligned values between an employee and an organization. If your values match, then think how committed they will be from the off.

New starters and induction

How are values communicated to new starters? How are they played out through the leadership? And then through their continued employment?

The principle that I am trying to highlight is that this stretches across multiple teams. Until you have broken this down into bite-sized practical chunks with owners and completion dates, you can't move into creating your communication plan, because you have no idea what you will be communicating as you have yet to build out the detail. You could launch the new values but then you're playing catch-up and immediately credibility is lost because it looks haphazard. If you are in recovery mode from a poor implementation first time round, then now more than ever this is the most critical part. Consider every element of the employee lifecycle and agree what needs to be adjusted to ensure the values are incorporated. What are the touchpoints to make this a continuous channel of *value* information?

Once you have your plan together with the detail boxed off, that's when you need to make a decision: do you go big bang, everything designed and ready for launch day or are you making small adjustments that you are going to communicate as you go? Either way, it's your decision as it has to be right for the business. What you should factor in is how you will communicate: what are the most effective communication channels for each population, are they tried and tested, and what is the feedback loop? Yes, feedback: how will you know what you are sending out is being received, *and* received and interpreted, in the way it was intended? With a comprehensive feedback loop you will know what is working and if you need to make any changes, you can. Be honest, be open, let your employees know that they can feed back – and they should. This has to work for them and if it doesn't and they can't use it then it's not effective. Listen to what they are saying because if you can't hear them, you are probably not having the impact you wanted to achieve. Feedback shows engagement; challenge shows you have passion. Listen to the people who want to challenge as they will become your foot soldiers in your ambitions.

This is not cultural change; this is cultural development (I've said it before and I will say it again!). It is the ongoing process of continually checking that you are making inroads in creating a great place to work.

It is the continuation of lacing your values in gold and creating the bedrock for your business. Consider the value of gold in this metaphor. Gold has long been a measure of value and wealth in numerous cultures. One of the most precious metals, gold is known for its superiority and purity, and is formidable under pressure. Be formidable, define your values, keep them pure and pressure test them; laced in gold, they are the foundations to build from.

5

The thread that binds us

The employee lifecycle

This chapter is a big one! Here we step away from the process of culture and move towards the human side of engagement, exploring each thread of the employee lifecycle. The chapter will provide you with the questions to review what impact your culture has on your employees, and what in practice might need to change to give you your desired culture. We will look at the issue of leadership capability and leaders' role in creating an aligned culture. Without acceptance and alignment with leadership capability then culture will be a project. There needs to be consistency within each thread of the journey; without this, the desired culture will soon unravel.

How your culture appeals to the labour market

Defining your culture answers the question about who you are as an employer and equally what it feels like to work in your organization. Does what you put out to the external world mirror the culture you aspire to have? Is there a seamless journey where the new employee transitions from the outside world to the inside world and does their perception remain the same?

Why this matters is that for years we have been talking about the *war for talent*. If you want to attract the best, you need to have a strong attraction strategy with a well-defined employer brand: one that showcases the true culture. For example, if you were to ask someone what it is like to work at Facebook, you can already guess the response. It's a well-known culture! Facebook is built on multiple acquisitions of small companies who were all entrepreneurial SMEs, so the ethos and value of self-development, drive and innovation runs through, connecting each business unit with the other.

Knowing your culture and being authentic to it makes attracting and recruiting aligned employees in the business seamless.

For the external world, create a content strategy that is aligned with your culture; this way, you have the right people wanting to join. There is zero point in pushing out team-building posts on social media and presenting your business in a way that shows inclusivity and innovation when the reality is the business is a top-down power hierarchy. You will be attracting people to your business who will have a short shelf life once they realize their wings have been clipped and their lips sealed shut.

Consider your approach and what will have most impact; corporate posts are good but the value of natural posts is significant. Posts that are written by the employee because they have been swept up in the moment and, yes, have been posted without corporate approval – now these mean something. They are a timely snapshot and give an insight into what the culture is really like.

Many businesses have grown their footprint on LinkedIn, a platform for showcasing your brand to the consumer, but it also gives insights for prospective employees about what it is like to work for the business. How many followers does your company page have? Are they following as a consumer or because they want to see what it is like to work in your company? Are your campaigns built for the consumer or the prospective employee? Or is there a balance? And does the tone of the campaigns match your company's culture?

Whatever your budget for marketing, people buy from people. If you can showcase your product or service alongside the people that make it happen then you are bringing your world to life. Businesses are nothing without people.

Once you have reviewed the employer brand, consider what more needs to be done: simplicity and consistency are key. Know what you want to say, say it and say it again.

Look at how the brand fits with your recruitment process. How are you validating that the people you are attracting and hiring fit with the culture you are creating?

The process of attracting and hiring the right people for your culture

Onboarding has become the buzz word over the last few years. The full kit and caboodle of attracting, recruiting and ultimately hiring a new employee. The cost of getting this right: increased performance, team morale and results. But the cost of getting it wrong is considerable.

As you move to your desired culture, the attributes and behaviours you want to see need to become a dominant factor in your recruitment process. To check your process against your culture, ask yourself the following:

- Do your job advertisements paint the real picture of what the role is and the company culture?
- Does the job title make sense? (An initial indicator of culture.)
- Are the job titles consistent? Do they make sense or have the hiring managers overinflated the role with a fancy new title?

I'm a big believer that to attract the widest population, a job title needs to say what it is. Even if it is a 'snake milker' – someone who milks snakes of their venom, or a 'chick sexer' – someone who determines the sex of chickens; however peculiar these job titles may seem, they accurately describe the jobs. There's no ambiguity; a snake milker knows what to look for, as that is his or her role title. It's the norm, and they would search accordingly. If we become too creative and advertise for a 'poison extraction artist' or a 'milk maid', we are not going to get the niche candidates we are looking for. So, take heed, hiring managers, recruitment love your creativity and boundless optimism but keep the titles in line with the business you are in and the role you are trying to recruit.

The content also has to reflect the responsibilities of the role. Now I get this is probably sounding very old hat, but in my experience, job descriptions that truly reflect the role and culture aren't always apparent. Ask HR to work with your stakeholder, ask a million questions, challenge them hard, tell them to prioritize the responsibilities. Make this a sure thing, not a fast thing.

The recruitment team needs to receive a job description that is accurate; it needs to have the right title and to have been benchmarked correctly. If not, then this is a disaster waiting to happen. Once the responsibilities have been ironed out, then you move on to the skills and behaviours required to fulfil this role. How aligned are these to the culture and values that have been identified? They should mirror them but be weighted towards the need of this particular role. If one of your values/competencies has been identified as 'collaboration' then don't contradict this within the behaviours. If the hiring manager states that this person needs to be the sole decision maker who needs to be able to work on their own to deliver exceptional results, then challenge how this role aligns with the culture you are trying to create. It may well do so, but collaboration must also happen at a point; this needs to be formally articulated so the golden thread keeps running.

Lastly, the sign-off process for the new role is a real cultural tell – is the process complex, too complex? Make the recruitment of your newest person into the business the simplest process in the book.

Preparing the candidate

Prime the candidate ready for a possible meeting. Contact needs to be made by the appropriate person, whether in an initial call, a direct invite to an interview itself or an assessment centre invite. Are you as a business acting as though this is a two-way process and is what you are putting out there truly indicative of who you are? Prospective employees will assess you as a business and should be as thorough as you are being with them. I cannot reiterate enough the waste of time, effort and cost if you get this wrong. Every candidate may also be an existing or prospective customer. I once worked in a business that had completely neglected this fact and ignored pools of people, choosing not to interact, not to provide feedback and essentially giving them poor insight into the mechanisms of the business. If this is how you choose to treat the people who may ultimately work for you, then how are you going to treat me as a customer? Remember, people talk with their feet.

But if you are a large business that can't possibly respond to every applicant, then make this known. Have an end date on your job advert; advise that if candidates don't hear back by a specified date then at this given time they have been unsuccessful, but that you thank them for their interest and you will keep them on record (given they have approved – thank you GDPR gods), and you'll be in touch should anything else arise. Go one step further and mail merge at the end of each week all the people you haven't corresponded with and send them a quirky email – make it fun – make it empathetic, wish them well in their job hunt and send a link to the development section on your website that provides advice to the job hunter, CV writing skills, hints and tips, interview techniques. You have just personalized an experience; you have given them support. And it may not have taken you any time. That candidate will remain or become a prospective customer; now that's a win. You turned a negative into a positive, you connected a lost connection, win-win.

You can repeat this with those who have been contacted this week and invited in. Send a similar email to them on the Friday:

> Congratulations, we've heard you've been invited in to meet with us. Please find some more information on who we are as a business, what our values our, what our culture is and if you need any support in your preparation, click here.

It's seamless, time efficient and provides the insights they need. Again, this is dependent on the type of business you are in, but my point is to review what you do. If you spend as much time looking at the employee lifecycle as the customer one and look at each thread to see if you are maximizing your relationship, then you will be in a different space. You need to balance consumer versus employee. Get it right and it will be magic. Get it wrong and it's costly, time consuming and in many cases infuriating all around.

Applicant tracking and cultural assessments

More and more businesses are moving towards cultural assessment testing, built directly into the Applicant Tracking System (ATS). This will only work if the business first knows what the culture of the organization is and, second, that it is honest and brave enough to go out there with it and immediately reduce the pool of talent that it is trying to access. It takes courage but what's the alternative: attract great talent who join, but then later realize that this is not for them or vice versa? The cost of mis-hiring is huge...

You can enhance your data gathering as we walk through each section as you'll gain further insights into the threads already in place in your culture and those that may need further attention.

- What is the average tenure in role?
- What are your attrition rates?
- In particular, what is your turnover in the first six months?

Are you getting it right in the hiring process or not? If you have a cultural assessment or a hiring committee, what does the success rate look like and does it predict performance? How close is it to reality? Check, check and double-check. If you have a system like this and it works then hats off to you, as this is a business dedicated to making sure the right person is hired not just for the job, but for the business, for everyone they will be working with. You have recruited with intent and that is magical.

If you're a business, however, that isn't getting it right then I suggest you review what you do. I'd strongly suggest you look first at the measures imposed on the resourcing function.

Recruitment cultural indicators

Cost to hire and time to hire: Both measures impact quality. Limited time and a 'bums on seats' attitude will result in average hires, or good hires that may not be culturally aligned. This can result in employee turnover, which increases costs.

But if you target 'quality hires' and have a team who understands the culture you are trying to achieve, then you have the making of a great hire, one here for the long term.

Ask yourself: How do you measure a quality hire, and how is this aligned with the culture you're trying to create?

It is also worth exploring whether you predict performance within your recruitment process. Have you defined what that predictor would be and tested it for accuracy?

In many organizations, the best predicator of performance is cognitive ability. Testing typically covers a wide range of aptitudes, including logical reasoning, verbal, computational, analytical skills and so on. Cognitive ability is well known as a key skill associated with problem solving, innovation and tenacity. You can see why this is a good predictor of performance.

So if your applicant scores highly on the cognitive test and the cultural assessment you have for your business, then it is far more likely that this employee will be a quality hire who is here to stay.

For example, in one client's business, the cultural assessment demonstrated that where candidates outperformed on the customer service focused questions, they went on to be their top performers. They also remained with the business 120% longer than other candidates. The client found this out by continually trialling their process.

If you haven't uncovered your predictor for performance, look at your data, your turnover, and start looking at the prevalent skills of those who are staying in the organization. What does that tell you already? And what do you need to do to alter your process to make it more effective?

Talent moves: Measuring talent moves within the business will indicate whether you are an organization that develops from within and whether you do it well with the right processes that set your people up for success.

All talent moves should be tracked: lateral, upwards, and so on. Are the talent moves successful? These must be true promotions or stretch assignments that showcase the ability of the individual and their effectiveness in the new role. If you uncover that you are moving people too quickly, or too slowly, what is this telling you about your culture?

Referral programme: Do you have a 'refer-a-friend' programme, and if so, what is the take-up? Is it effective? Is it ineffective? Is it ineffective because no one would recommend this organization or is it just unknown? What are the trends in each functional area?

A strong business that puts a great onus on its people will have a strong refer-a-friend scheme – beneficial to the employee, the business and prospective employee. The best schemes in the world will not be accessed if the business doesn't care for its employees. Your employees will be looking for the exit door, certainly not the door for them to open and invite their friends through.

Leaders recognize this is not an HR problem but an intrinsic business issue that goes back to the question earlier posed: 'Would you recommend xxx as a great place to work?' What is an acceptable number of positive responses here, because if this doesn't come back as 100% then you're doing something wrong and need to understand why. You don't see surgeons saying: 'As long as seven out of my ten operations today are successful then that's OK, right?' No, it's clearly not right as it would mean three people have just undergone something significant and it didn't work out; imagine if you are one of the three awaiting surgery for something particularly serious that results in further harm, and to your utter horror it's all ok from the hospital's perspective as they allow a 30% failure rate.

My point is to know who you are and who you are recruiting. Create an environment where people want to join. Be known as a place that gets the current challenges within society and build a culture that people want to be part of. Your biggest and most effective attraction strategy is through referrals. Commercially, it's a smidge of the cost of hiring externally, and culturally, who knows your business better?

You, or a recruitment agency? Unless they absolutely know your business inside-out, how do you know you are going to get the right fit?

This section should have provided you with some real tangible data that you can reflect on. How has what you learnt showcased how close you are to the culture you want, and how the people you are attracting into your business are aligned to your aspirant culture?

Are you a referral-built business, is your focus on quality or are you in a business that is working at such pace that it's just about hitting the numbers? If it is the latter, what is the impact? Look long term, look at the churn. Short-term immediacy can only go so far; there are only so many people available, the laws are changing and skills shortages will become more prevalent. How are you future-proofing your business?

The interview

One of the biggest moments in a prospective employee's career is the interview. It shapes their future but also their perceptions of how you treat your employees, which in turn gives them a personal perspective on your company's culture.

Get the basics right: provide the details and make sure they are accurate. Provide parking details, if required. If there are parking costs, tell them. If there are access challenges, tell them. Make sure both the candidate and the hiring manager have the information they need. You may be the coolest cucumber but being sent inaccurate information or being obstructed in any way can only enhance what can be an anxious day.

Things can go wrong, and we can all be late, but it should be near on unacceptable for the hiring manager to be late. If it can't be helped by either party, then explain. Do not leave your candidate waiting in some foyer while you are filled with your own self-importance. The hiring manager and the culture of the organization are being presented, and should be under as much scrutiny as the potential candidate is to you.

If you can't arrive on time to welcome the candidate, then what level of support will you be offering them once they have joined the business? Nada! Little! Maybe some, but if you really want talent in your business, then treat candidates as you expect to be treated. Create the right experience, be fully present and make the right first impression. This is important because if they are talent, they will be deciding which business and culture is right for them. They will have more than one job offer; blow this and they will opt for the other organization who treated them with respect, and who could blame them?

The experience you provide through the recruitment process will sell you as the hiring manager and the culture of the business tenfold. I have watched the most genteel of managers turn into ogres: the interview experience they give not being dissimilar to that of a waterboarding exercise. It was brutal and nothing like what it was actually like to work at the company or their real style as a manager. When I challenged the manager about their style and what they thought it achieved, they responded with: 'I wanted to see how they respond under pressure.' I get that, but there are ways to do this that don't have the candidate running so quickly in the opposite direction that they would give Usain Bolt a run for his money. What they created was a scenario that wasn't a true representation of the company's culture.

Alternatively, you may be in a business where ogres, and that approach, is the culture – in which case, it's authentic. You have presented the culture to the candidate and they have a choice to decide whether this is business that culturally aligns with the one they want to be in.

As a side note, please remember this is an experience; make sure you conduct the interview in a room – and no, the canteen isn't acceptable. If you have offices, use one, but be mindful to what's in it and where it is located. I experienced an interview once where a disciplinary was taking place in the room next door. The disciplinary was clearly not being handled well, and soon escalated. With the voices getting louder and louder, the din was deafening. The candidate was being expected to continue while profanities about the management being sh*t were being bellowed next door. Stop, apologize and move the candidate, and offer some form of explanation. All may not be lost if you are honest about the culture as it stands, and why you are bringing in new blood. People are understanding; we all get that nowhere is perfect, so it's your role to be transparent and show authenticity.

Introduction

You have a room, everything is set up, no confidential information is on show, the last candidate's information is already stored away, they are comfortable and you have offered them a drink. These are basic manners; it's like inviting someone into your home, making them feel welcome and put at ease. If you just fling a tirade of questions at them without putting them at ease, chances are you'll not get the real person. Instead, they will give you the answers they think you want to hear. When you put people at ease, they open up and give you more. You don't want rehearsed, robotic answers; you want them to bring their true, authentic selves. It is then that you will know if they really have what it takes to meet the needs of the job. You can also make a decision about whether or not this person fits the culture.

Welcome them and thank them for coming. Don't immediately dive into your interview booklet but connect with them: ask how they are and how they found getting here – a simple but effective way of seeing if they have experienced any blockers that already may have hampered their desire to work with you, or at this location. Then lead into the interview by asking what they know about your business and what in particular attracted them to this role. Listen to what they are really saying. Recent research identified that roughly 5%

of decisions are made within the first minute and 30% within five minutes.[1] This is terrifying; we need to explore the speed of that decision and how that decision was made. More on this in a minute, but the point here is, if this is you, and you make decisions with your gut, or you have hiring managers who do this, are they recruiting like for like? Or are they that engrained in the culture they know immediately what they are looking for? Either way, create the environment so that the candidate does all the talking, so that you are the most informed to be able to make a rational decision.

When talking through the role with the candidate, don't oversell or undersell the role else there will be a complete mismatch. Again, this is about knowing the business you're in, its culture and finding the person who can help take it forward. If the role doesn't have Profit and Loss responsibility or they don't set their own budget, don't sit there telling them they can run it like their own business. It's clear they can't and they will have been misled. They will start a role that they have been mis-sold, soon realizing that with the limits put on them they will be playing solely with numbers they have no say in. They will soon become frustrated with a role they have no autonomy in.

Undersell a role and some might feel underwhelmed. If you have done the work upfront on the job description, accurately detailing the roles and responsibilities, with an advert that shows the candidate what they are, then all that is left is to make sure the hiring manager can articulate the role in a clear and concise way, and bring a *'day in the life'* into real context. Highlight the complexity they may need to navigate: the pitfalls, the opportunities, the real challenges/learning experiences from the last incumbent. Make this process a reality.

---

[1] P. Harris, 'Study: How quickly do interviewers really make decisions?' Workopolis, 2015. Available from https://careers.workopolis.com/ advice/study-how-quickly-do-interviewers-really-make-decisions/amp [accessed 8 January 2021].

Question stage

Next, the question stage. You have a suite of competency-based questions built from the competencies you have chosen as a business or from the values. Either way, is what you are trying to achieve here aligned with the culture you're trying to create? Make this known; educate your hiring managers. Managers need to know what behaviours the business wants to see; otherwise, they will be employing technically competent people who might not be aligned in the slightest. It is a great way of sharing with the candidate that the competencies you have just been discussing are those that this business is built on. Ask the candidate: 'Do you have any concerns? Are there any areas you think you might need support with?' Be open; these are not a secret. The secret here is make no secret of them; be open, you will get more.

Once the more formal questions have been answered and you have talked about the role, ask the candidate about which working relationship with a line manager they enjoyed the most and why. You will learn so much from this and their response will give a clear indicator about whether they will work well with you and how culturally aligned they are with your company. Be open; discuss the type of manager you are and what your expectations are of your team.

Then ask them the real questions: 'What gets you up in the morning? What does a bad day look like? What is your definition of hard work? If you had your own business, what role would your take on?'

There are so many questions that tap into the emotional drivers of an individual. Yes, asking them to describe their strengths and weaknesses is great, but you want to know more than that. You want to know how they have identified their strengths and weaknesses, and what they do to enhance and protect those skills. These questions will give you a greater understanding of their level of self-awareness; if they have self-awareness in abundance, then it is highly likely that their personal development will be high on their agenda. A candidate who wants to continually develop is gold: they are seeking a higher level, intellectually, socially and emotionally. They are the candidate who will drive a culture where the ego is removed and there's a bigger purpose: if it's for the greater good of everyone, it's for the greater good of the business. Finally, mix your questions up. I was recruiting for a trainer a good few years ago and always ended on three questions.

1. *Can you tell me ten things you can do with an orange?* I wanted to see the level of creativity and ingenuity.
2. *Can you tell me a joke?* Trainers/facilitators have to think on their feet; they need to be able to handle everything that is thrown at them in a training room. I didn't need a fall-off-your-seat-laughing joke, although that was always a bonus. I needed to see how they handled a curve ball, particularly if they went blank; it was the handling of going blank I wanted to see, the credibility of handling the request effectively and with a touch of style.
3. *If your life was a movie, what actor would play you?* Always insightful. Try this out; it gives you an insight into how the person sees themselves – you get to see their life through their lens. My all-time favourite was when a candidate said within a blink of an eye 'Arnie Schwarzenegger'. He then went on to explain why, and at 6ft 5 his explanation was understandable. We wrapped up the interview and just as he got to the door, he turned around, and with a raise of the eyebrow and a damn near-perfect accent said, 'I'll be back...' Obviously, he got the job. He was quick-thinking, charismatic and could convey a message. He was culturally aligned with the business and particularly the function he was joining.

Wrap up

Finally, give the candidate plenty of time to ask you or the hiring manager questions. This is where they have fully relaxed, so keep your focus. What questions are they asking? What indicators are they giving you that they meet the culture of your business?

Interviewing is a skill; it is emotional intelligence in abundance. Great leaders, and I mean leaders, those that can really lead and empower their teams to deliver results, by nature will already be exceptional interviewers. They know what they are looking for; they know the make-up of their team and each member will be different but will complement the rest of the team. The culture will be strong with or without a defined organizational culture because that leader has built it on trust, respect and with high emotional intelligence.

Review the above and the capabilities of your hiring managers. Are they presenting the culture in a way that begins the new employees' journey in the right way? This is the start of the process and a doorway to the culture of your business; they are the gatekeepers. If you are giving them that responsibility, then do so wisely.

All interviews concluded, the same questions asked each time, marking has taken place, there has been no bias, and you are making your decision based on a sound numerical outcome. It may be coupled with the outcome of a cultural assessment, it may be that the person just felt right; however that decision was made, your role here is to review consistency.

If 'hiring committees' are in your business then this takes time and commitment. It needs to be a well thought through process and to happen at speed, with the 'committee' having the final say. This can be seen as a tougher and longer process but it does it give you what you need from a culture alignment perspective.

Review your process, and make sure that however you ask the questions, you are showing the candidate what it is like to be part of your team, and part of your business, so they can then make their decision. They can then decide whether this is the right business for them. Is this a place where they can belong?

Belonging is paramount, and a topic that is becoming increasingly high on everybody's agenda as it is intrinsically linked with mental wellbeing. Joining a business should feel like you have found that safe haven. A place you can call home. A place that will wrap its arms around you, rather than invoke anxiety in you. Create a toxic environment and watch your absence rates hike. Create a culture of inclusivity, focused on the welfare of its people, and you will have created loyalty. You may have created a place where for the first time in some people's lives they feel like they have somewhere to turn. If the greater good of the business is to look after its people, that business will flourish. The world is changing; toxic businesses are being outperformed by businesses with a deeper purpose and where people feel connected.

Acceptance or rejection

When the candidate says 'Yes', celebrate with them and ask how they feel about handing in their notice. Do they need any support or guidance? They may not, but consider how thoughtful that offer was. It has meaning; you are showing up for them and are continuing to build a relationship. And if they turn down your job offer, be dignified, part ways in the best possible way, but find out why. What was it that the other company or leader had that tipped the decision? This is intelligence you need. Are you gathering insights such as how many offers are rejected per week, and why? And what are you doing with that information? If it is about the ogre interviewer, then tell them. Share with the interviewer that being something that they're not has resulted in a loss. Be honest and help them develop.

If it was because the package wasn't where it needed to be, you can check the benchmarking but the reality is more and more people are turning towards companies with wellbeing at their heart, authentic cultures and better prospects.

Another top reason is that people want an opportunity to grow. Are you as a business giving them that opportunity; do your leaders see the importance in truly knowing what people want? And knowing themselves how to sell it to potential employees? Do your hiring managers recognize that they need to be selling themselves and the business as much as the candidate is selling their skills and experiences?

If you are in a business that has got this right, you're there; the recruitment team or the hiring manager have offered the position and you're keeping the employee warm – with three months as a notice period and sometimes up to six. Keeping the lines of communication open is vital in showcasing who you are as an employer.

You are nurturing the start of a relationship and one which you want to last, so keep talking. If a change in the business happens that may impact them, make sure you share that nugget of information. There is nothing worse than a new candidate having read some extract in the news (potential acquisition, job losses) without wider context. Engage with them directly. Even if it doesn't impact them, they might feel it does as they know no different, so support them. Give them the answers before they raise the questions.

Keep them excited; make them feel like they are the most important addition to the business, because they are. If you have got this right, then as a leader your job just got easier as your team is strengthening with the right talent that will allow you to push forward to work closer to the ultimate business goal. Invite them in for coffee, arrange a Zoom meeting, get them together with their new team. Keep the excitement going.

We have all moved house. We have all experienced the turbulence of looking at numerous houses until we find the 'one'. The one we want to call *home*. We are about to subject ourselves to a lifelong mortgage with excruciating payments. We have navigated the reams of paperwork, the insurance, the payslips, then, anticipating the joy of about to move, we find out that someone along the chain has had an emergency involving their cocker spaniel. All of a sudden, the chain is touch and go; unless everyone can push the move date back a day, then the move is off... yes this happened, bloody cocker (I take that back, I love dogs). It's frustrating, anxiety inducing, paper laden, intoxicatingly difficult and then it happens, finally move day takes place and we're in our new home at last, and it's all been worth it. We have achieved what we set out to do. We are in our home that we have painfully worked for. And as we sit back and reflect, we realize we are spending a whopping four awake hours a day in this house experiencing the fruits of our labour. Four! A measly four while we are spending the other twelve hours of our day at work, commuting, followed by dropping off and picking kids up from school. We are spending two and a half times longer in the working environment and not at the home we have just lost blood, sweat and tears over. If we want to be happy, we need to be confident that the workplace is one that really supports who we are and that culturally it's a perfect match.

The long run

Validate that your new employees' experience is aligned with the culture you are shaping. Ask the following:

- Did you know what it would be like to work here before you started?
- How aligned is what you thought the culture of the business was like before you joined with what the actual culture is like now you work here?
- If not, what misalignments are there?
- Where could we improve the experience?

What are the gaps you identified? What improvements can you make? This is you holding the mirror to shaping the right process and experience for all future employees of your business.

If the hire doesn't work out, what do the behaviours of the hiring manager show? Do they reflect on what they now deem as the 'bad hire'? 'I knew they wouldn't work out; I should have gone with my gut.' Why do managers need to prove a point – to reassert that they are so intellectually astute they predicted that this individual wasn't going to meet the required standards for them to fulfil the role?

No... this says nothing about their intellectual prowess, nor does their intuition need its own job title. Interviewing involves ploughing your time and that of the resourcing function into interviewing multiple people until you find the person that matched the role at hand. Your 'gut feeling' was a physiological reaction to something that was said or not said – something resonated with you. This was your gut giving you a sign; it was telling you to explore further, to ask the candidate the question: 'Tell me more about that,' 'If you could develop any skill, which would it be?' or simply, 'Is this an area you wish to feel more confident in, what would you need to build your confidence?' Or to just use the power of silence to seek out where that disruption came from.

Organizations that strive for a culture of openness and inclusivity build the relationship from the beginning based on open two-way dialogue. Questions are asked to support people, not to catch them out! These businesses ask questions with true intent, such as: 'If you were the successful candidate and we could support you in developing that skill further, what would the impact of that be?' The hiring manager gains insights into how receptive the potential new employee is to continual development. They have uncovered whether they have a growth mindset. And the candidate has found a prospective employer who has already said they will invest in them. An employer who has allowed them to be vulnerable, who provided them with the time and opportunity to show the area which may have been deemed by others as a weakness. Instead of using it against them, they have used it as a vehicle to build trust. This is the start of what will become a very well-formed relationship in an open culture.

Recruitment is a vital part of the process to ensure cultural continuity. This is where you lay the foundations of acceptable and unacceptable forms of behaviour, which in turn create the culture you have. Execute this well and already the standard has been set. Build trust and you have a new starter who will be comfortable to ask the questions to clarify that they are performing as they should be. If you identified a development area within the recruitment process and weave it into their inductions, then you have straightaway shown commitment and continuity of process – a process that puts that individual's needs before anything else. That's a manager leading a culture where support and development is in place for you to be the best you can be.

Benefits

The benefits of being part of your organization, as we know, are showcased at the job advertisement stage. Due to its complexity, the emotiveness of the subject and the sheer disparity between who gets what within an organization, we need a section dedicated to it.

The benefits package and who it applies to is a clear *cultural indicator*. It will further impact how people will respond in the business and how they behave. Do your benefits instil the culture you want, or are your benefits driving the wrong behaviour?

Edgar Schein talked about assumptions; when looking at your benefits, consider the assumptions made by the employees – long-standing assumptions that may be causing animosity within your teams. Are the benefits consistent? Or, have they become fragmented over time, as different leaders create benefit ecosystems that disrupt and impact other teams?

For example, if you had a benefit system that rewarded silo behaviour and you want to move towards a *Collaborate* culture, your benefits won't align. I have seen a sales team who were rewarded on personal targets only. It drove a behaviour where supporting each other wasn't considered, as that would only detract employees from doing their own tendering and potential sales. The result was an initial spike in performance which soon dipped. Team development became stifled and peer-on-peer development was non-existent. The team, and I say that loosely, along with their sales, became stagnant.

Would team targets and collective bonuses create a different dynamic? Culturally collective performance would support the shift to a new culture if you were looking to have a more collaborative culture.

Let's start with the basic benefits. Who within your organization can access the following: private medical care, flexible benefits, dental treatment, gym membership, PPE, wellbeing access, employee assistance programme, access to buying holiday time, access to selling holiday time; an online portal inclusive of all of that and shopping discounts? Do the benefits fit the needs of the employee and what distinguishing factors are there about who receives what (e.g. level of seniority, pay grade, contract type)?

Please don't – While we are on the topic of standard benefits, consider this point. You have an office role, you get a laptop and mobile; as a business, please refrain from selling that as a benefit. I can assure you that being accessible 24/7 is not a benefit in any way, shape or form; it's a necessity for the job, but not a benefit.

Ask yourself and your employees: Are the benefits you're promoting and providing those that support the target culture? Get back to the grassroots, talk to your people, and find out what would make a difference to the behaviours you are seeing being rewarded.

There are businesses who have already introduced 'me' days, 'have your birthday off' days, 'voluntary charity days off' and 'pet days' based on their findings from talking to their people. Boutique businesses whose benefits reflect who they are really work. These businesses have an attractive purpose, particularly for our millennials and Generation Zs. Offering aligned benefits that build on that purpose makes them even more attractive.

As with all things culture, know what is important to the employees and what would serve the culture best, and break the mould. Too often, current employee benefit schemes appear tired, the same benefits available year on year. Be original, be dynamic, have benefits that have meaning because you have listened to your people and they support your target culture.

Next, *communicate*! Too many businesses have sourced incredible benefits, yet they have failed in their communications to reach their employees.

The benefits and wellbeing of your employees should not be a tick-box exercise: benefits portal launched, new uniform available, refer-a-friend scheme launched. Whatever the benefits are, if your employees don't know about them, you have formulated them for all the wrong reasons and what is presented at board level is a list of accomplishments, but for whom? What should be presented to the board are benefit take-ups, adoption of the services; what are the trends saying? What are you doing next to flex the benefits in line with the themes? And how are the benefits supporting the behavioural shift towards your target culture?

Be as interested in the services you are providing to your employees as you are in the service you are giving your customers. What is the cost per annum for a loss of a single customer? What is the cost per person for the loss of an employee? Cost leadership should be inclusive of employee engagement as that has an impact on the customer. And lastly, track how your benefits support your cultural agenda.

Pay

One of the key threads in the employee lifecycle, pertinent to the employee, is the wage check. A potentially contentious topic, as it's hard to have a price put on your head. This is a thread that should be reviewed; it has cultural impact.

Organizations where pay bands are either non-existent, subjective, or are there but with a lack of transparency, are highly likely to have managers within the same business who operate pay inconsistently. The impact? Disgruntled employees. We know that, because despite the clause in the contract stating the confidentiality required around pay, people talk.

Where organizations are transparent with salary bands, have equality of pay and remove the subjectivity around individuals' pay, then everyone knows where they are, what to expect and when. The pay is reflective of the job that person will be fulfilling, not the individual's negotiation ability. Having the structure in place opens doorways to employees to grow their responsibilities in a clear way. It also opens doorways to those who wish to lessen their responsibilities should they decide they have reached a point where they want to step back. In doing so, there is a clear framework in place for a job change, the salary adjusted in line with the new responsibilities and pressure, new expectations are set and role creep is reframed. This should be seen as a positive because you have kept someone who needed a change but was too valuable to lose, and the contentious issue and backlash has gone.

You might be in an organization where the fine art of Picasso is replicated in your *red circling* antics. The changing of someone's role, but maintaining their existing salary and benefits. This is seen as a way to keep hold of people you don't want to lose, but where their role is no longer of the scale to warrant the salary. This process can and does have an impact on culture. I've seen first hand individuals who have had some of their responsibilities removed: they were initially aggrieved but then overcame this, happily sharing the news that they now don't need to do all those hours but still get paid the same. The wider impact? Damaging.

So, the question we must ask is why did the business choose to do this? Typically, when we get to the root of this, the organization acknowledges that it hasn't been fair. They have overpromoted without support; their line manager didn't provide the development they needed; or maybe they could see where the employee was going wrong, and never had the courage to provide real feedback. 'Hey, these are the things that need improving; can you do this? What do you need from me to make that happen? OK great, let's review.' It isn't hard yet we still have cultures where people are afraid to give feedback. So instead of feedback, your red *circle action* has just cost the business a collision with the culture you're trying to create.

Pay: Division of labour

One of the more contentious issues, particularly within ware-house/manufacturing businesses, is where senior leaders are taking 40% bonuses while 'workers on the ground' are grappling with a 1.5% pay rise. The argument always being, 'How is this fair?' The simple answer to this is, it's not. However you look at this, this is a cultural deviation. We want to look after our people, we have flexible benefits, but we pay minimum wage.

Post-Brexit restrictions imposed on 'skilled workers' will mean it is going to get harder to recruit into 'blue-collar roles', so if this is your arena and culture is your thing then defining who you want to be as an employer will be critical in stabilizing a fluid market. The pond you're fishing in will only get smaller so reducing churn has to be a number-one priority.

In a society where we still distinguish 'white-collar' and 'blue-collar' workers, consider what you call your employees/colleagues/associates. Be clear about what labels you are putting on your people. To be labelled is to be given an identity – one which can ultimately be self-limiting.

Alfred Adler (1870–1937), Austrian medical doctor and psychologist and founder of the school of individual psychology, introduced the concept of 'division of labour' within communities, and that we all have a role to fulfil. This can be applied to the workplace, with all forms of work being of equal value. Adler also stated that 'A person's worth is decided by the *way* in which they fulfil their role is assigning the division of labour in their community.'[2] In other words, someone's worth isn't determined by the type of work they engage in. It is decided by the attitude with which they undertake that work.

In the workplace, all the roles you employ should be necessary to fulfil your purpose; without them *all*, you will incur challenges so value each role.

What are the cultural indicators in how the pay and benefits are shaped? How do they reflect the culture? What are the naming conventions used to call your employees? Your functions even? HR, is it still called human resources (god, it's an appalling name of a function – resources for humans, could it be any more robotic?) or is it called 'the people service team'? Whatever things are called and whatever the benefits are, what do they say about the culture you are trying to achieve?

Recognition

Let's first look at the psychological impact of recognition on an individual. When recognition is provided, the hypothalamus

---

[2] 'Alfred Adler (1870–1937): Individual psychology'. Available from https://study.sagepub.com/sites/default/files/Alfred%20Adler.pdf [accessed 18 January 2021].

and dopamine receptors are affected. The hypothalamus is the part of your brain that controls basic bodily functions, such as eating and sleeping, while dopamine releases the chemical that causes happiness and combats depression. Regular releases of dopamine can improve both quality of work and productivity.

If you were to ask individuals in your organization if they received recognition, what proportion of your workforce would say 'regularly', and what proportion would say, 'If I hear nothing, then I know I'm doing OK'?

The value and impact of a well-recognized workforce is an increase in trust, openness and effective team working. It provides a sense of security and employees value that their contribution is helping to achieve the business goals.

How often do you hear the words 'thank you' and going a little deeper, how often do you hear 'thank you' being said with true meaning and supported with context? 'Jo, what you did on that piece of work was remarkable, you added real value to the project, your contribution was excellent, thank you.'

Are people within your organization truly valued for their contribution? Do they know the value they bring and are they able to accept the recognition and use it to propel them forward? This isn't just about aligning recognition with your target culture; it is simply addressing this question: 'Are you meeting your employees' basic human needs?'

You can of course go one step further and review your recognition scheme (if you have one). Do you have an online system where people can recognize each other and say thank you? Has the process worked or has it become a time-consuming activity that is blocking the effect of a simple and direct 'thank you'? And how effective was its implementation? If people didn't say thank you to each other in person before, what development did you give your people to change their behaviour? No system could ever achieve that alone.

Large organizations are likely to ask this question in their engagement survey: 'Do you feel your contributions are valued?' First, asking this annually seems ludicrous and, second, the employee doesn't know who by: is the question asking whether they feel valued and recognized for their efforts by their line manager, or by the business? Remember, people leave poor managers not organizations, but equally you can have a great manager who recognizes effort but if this isn't recognized by the wider function or business, it will permeate through.

Look at your approach to recognition. Are you a culture that openly recognizes the value and contribution of your teams? What are the behaviours used to demonstrate appreciation and recognition in the business? Do you have leaders who see this as a core part of their role or do you need to review the process and the skills within the business to make improvements?

Joining the business: The induction

Your induction process can have a profound effect on your new starter. Not only will the experience shape their thinking about the organizational culture, but it will also resonate at a much deeper, personal level.

We have seen major changes in society: the surge of the digital era, the rise of the smartphone, virtual reality, artificial intelligence. We are evolving exponentially and yet the impact on our wellbeing has never been so paramount; we have become more connected digitally, but less connected emotionally. Couple these emotional needs with the fallout of a pandemic and there is a far greater need now than before to provide your people with a sense of 'belonging'.

We have a basic human need to belong, to connect, to see the light in each other's eyes when we talk, to see the ripples of laughter running across our faces, the friendships that allow us to show and bare our souls, knowing that true friendship means no judgement, the safety of another.

As you shape your culture, consider whether your business is built on one purpose: to succeed. Or, two purposes: to succeed and create a sense of belonging for each employee. What if the importance is placed on both running concurrently? What would that business look like? What would the culture be?

I previously likened the recruitment process to showcasing a 'window to the culture' of the business. The next stage, however, the induction process, is like opening the door wide and inviting new starters in.

Stay with me here: You've been invited to a friend's house for the first time, they provided you with a time that suited you both, directions to make sure the journey was as easy as possible, and details of where to park. You were greeted in the nicest of ways. You were set at ease immediately. You followed your host through to a large open-plan kitchen; it was decorated well, you felt comfortable. Your host offers you a drink and as they make the drink, they inform you to make yourself at home, and you do. Your drink along with a host of nibbles are put in front of you and it makes the conversation flow; you're at ease.

Do you have a culture with a 'host' mentality? Have you created a culture where your new starters feel like they have just made the best decision of their life? Have they been greeted, talked to, engaged with and instantly put at ease? By putting your new starters at ease, they will be more willing to ask the questions they may hold back if they feel they are in an environment with no time to talk.

I worked on a project where we sent leaders to work with a charity organization that was resettling families of refugees in the UK. The leaders met the refugees at Birmingham Airport; they had flown in from France, having just left the Calais Jungle. The children of the families had grown up entirely in the refugee camps. After the leaders met with them, and with the charity, they travelled with them to the medical centre for their immunizations before they then went on to support rehousing.

When the leaders regrouped later that evening, emotions were high. In the excitement of the day, the leaders were talking over each other with explanations of what they saw, the feelings they had, the unanswered questions. We gave them time to reflect on what they had seen and to share what moved them the most. John, one of the leaders, shared how taken aback he was that the organization had to teach the family how to use windows. He then went on to share the impact of what we take for granted. The team reflected further and then we asked: 'What are the learnings you can take from this and adopt in the workplace?' You could have heard a pin drop and then one of the team likened the experience to joining a new business. Precisely! We agreed that it should never be as daunting, but people join businesses for many reasons and can be filled with apprehension.

The principle is the same; we take for granted the experience of joining a new business, of walking into a new building on your first day, knowing no one, and being stripped of everything you have ever known. You may have been at mastery stage in your old company; you knew everyone and everyone knew you. Now you may have changed sector, it may be a completely different job – whatever the reason for that role change, you have stepped out of your comfort zone. There will be those who thrive on moments like these, hungry for every morsel of information, using their sheer curiosity to seek out information. Ego gone, they capitalize on being the new person, knowing that no question is a daft one. Then there are those who may be more introspective; they sit quietly, absorbing everything they hear, saying less but reflecting. Whichever their style, you have a role to play. Provide them with an experience that allows them to embrace their first day and to leave feeling eager to return tomorrow.

The impact of a poor induction impacts not just on the new employee, but on the team that this role is moving into. The new person doesn't know their role, judgements can be made; the fallout of the team picking up a role that has been stagnant means that now the new person doesn't get the business. Honeymoon, what honeymoon? The cracks are already there; there may have been that gut feeling but as we see with so many people, there is an overwhelming desire to rectify this and make it work. With all good intent and purpose, effort is spilled into every interaction but try as they might the culture isn't what the new starter expected and slowly reality hits.

Litmus test this; ask your new starters for their induction plans. Are they standardized, is there a simple process of activity that everyone experiences, is there a host of events that take place so the new starter understands the business, the function and the culture of the business?

The induction process will give new starters a clear indication of the culture of the organization. If you have a learning culture, then undoubtedly you have empowered your new employee from the minute they joined to absorb the experience and enjoy the learning process. You are creating a culture where your employees crave to learn and have the freedom to think. An organization where the new starter leaves each day feeling like they have joined an organization that will allow them to grow. If you create an induction that provides your new starters with a chance to show their true self, to share their past experiences to connect on a deeper level, it shows that the induction process is two way – that you are as keen to learn as much from your new starters as they need to learn about you and the business.

People who want to do the right thing, who want to work with purpose, will re-evaluate their choices. Review the impact of your induction. If you were a new starter today, in your own business, would it work for you? Is it creating the culture you want it to? Failure to establish what the culture is in the induction will impact the perceptions of the employees. Therefore, look at the process and the alignment it has with the culture you are creating.

What depth is there to your induction?

Have a look at the following and consider whether your induction includes all the components you need to give a rounded welcome to your new starter:

- **Social** (the heart): The induction provides the welcome that introduces the new starter to all the right people. It provides a network; technical access to social communities. It shows the company journey, the values, the culture you aspire to have.
- **Knowledge and skills** (mind): Broken down, the induction content aligns with the job description. It includes the educational and learning components that will set the new starter up to succeed. Your new employee understands their roles and responsibilities and knows how to fulfil them.
- **Business context** (joining the dots): The induction is designed to help the new employee to join the dots. It highlights the role and its impact on wider teams. The role is explained in context to the team's purpose and how that fits into the organizational goals and purpose.
- **Expectations** (two way): The new employee has the opportunity to fully bring themselves to the table; they have been encouraged to ask the questions they really want the answers to. They know what is expected from them, behaviourally, targets, deliverables, and the relationship they will have with their line manager and the team. They have had the opportunity to share their own experiences. Don't neglect this: shared experiences forge strong relationships. They already feel like they belong and the culture and experience they were shown in the recruitment process continues, the bind of the golden thread deepening.

Lastly, review the accountability of the induction. It is a major *cultural tell.* Is it owned by the line manager? Or is owned by A N Other, as the line manager is too busy? What messaging are you putting out? Basic assumptions will be made and they are a critical factor in the make-up of culture. What time is truly committed to making your new starters feel a sense of belonging?

Health and wellbeing

Health and wellbeing should be a critical factor in organizations. If this isn't high up on your agenda, a compelling reason for why it should be is the report published by Deloitte in January 2020; they stated that poor mental health costs UK employers £45 billion each year, a rise of 16% since January 2016.[3] The second compelling reason should be if you are in charge of employees, then do everything to make them feel safe.

When shaping the culture of the organization or reviewing the existing culture you have, this is where the big questions must be asked.

- At what cost is the health and wellbeing of your employees?
- What pressure is too great?
- What environment do you want to create, and can you give your employees a 'safe word'? (I know! I totally stole that from *Fifty Shades,* but it's not a bad idea. A word you give to your employees so that if they ever feel out of their comfort zone or the pressure is too great, or something is going on at home, whatever the

---

[3] Deloitte, 'Poor mental health costs UK employers up to £45 billion a year'. Available from www2.deloitte.com/uk/en/pages/press-releases/articles/poor-mental-health-costs-uk-employers-up-to-pound-45-billion-a-year.html [accessed 18 January 2021].

reason, they can just say that word. It's simple. It means I need to talk but I can't find the words...)

- How important is the safety, security, health and well-being of your employees to your business?
- What measures have you put in place to protect your employees?
- Presenteeism is a heavy contributor to cost within the workplace, with many employees just 'showing up'. Do your employees feel safe to be absent with mental health? With the leap towards remote working, presenteeism has further increased burnout, with employees feeling like they are never 'off'. How are you creating an environment that allows people to be 'off', guilt free?

I'm sure there are more; take the time to look at the data available to you and calculate the cost of stress-related absence to you as a business. Is this a cost you can absorb or is it time for change? For those that believe having an employee assistance programme is an excuse to put people under relentless pressure and feel like you have adequately supported them – it's not.

And look at key words in your employee value proposition or in your job advertisements. Is there a theme of resilience or tenacity coming through? Challenge the business as to why this is an occurring theme. Is it down to volume and diversity of challenge or is it because you are employing one person to do a two-person job? This is not resilience or tenacity; you are employing on the basis of goodwill and that will run out.

This your time to consider how the wellbeing of your people fits with the culture you desire. What approach do you want to take? Review your organizational development. Consider whether a 'time in motion' study is needed to review what's expected at role level. Are more roles required or is there an overlap of responsibilities that could be altered?

Do you need to consider what level of training you want to provide your teams with? How do you ensure you employ and train people with emotional awareness, awareness to identify their own triggers, or triggers in others? What development do you provide to support them to help them deal with it?

In the report cited above, Deloitte shared that on average for every £1 spent on supporting employees' mental health, employers get £5 back from presenteeism, absenteeism and reduced absence. Early intervention and organizational education equate to a higher return in investment than if the employee is left and then needs longer-term support at a later date.

We have seen the value of 'Mental Health First Aiders' in business; it is a great step forward but cannot be done in isolation. The communication and engagement around these individuals and their importance must land effectively. It must be coupled with the education and development of all of your employees and the management education around the culture of what is acceptable and what is not. Only then will they land with purpose.

A period of poor mental health does not define an individual. Be the business that is eradicating this perception. Become a place where people can bring their authentic self and see the results. Face the challenges and do so with speed, because ultimately by protecting your people you are protecting your business.

There is a moral duty here. If you are implementing strategies that are for the purpose of making your employees work harder or to improve the perception of your employer brand, then it will have a negative impact on your employees. Instead, create a place where people not only belong but provide them with a safety net. Give people the courage to fall and know they are going to be caught.

Role of the manager/leader

This is one of the most crucial roles in business. Managers account for around 70% of the variance in a team's engagement and they are largely responsible and a key influencer in the wellbeing of their employees. It is largely known but often ignored that people leave managers not companies.

Where managers manage differently across the business, where what is acceptable in one team is not in another, then you have already diluted the team's focus. The team is now spending a proportion of its time dissecting the differences in the lack of equality. Productivity is lost and motivation dips. There's a commercial impact again. In some teams there will be nuances but there needs to be a rationale for that, which needs to be explained and understood. So often when working from home requests were submitted (before it became the norm), the difference in response would lead to comments such as: 'My manager doesn't trust that when I work from home, I actually work.' A team without trust is not a team; if you have little trust in your business and how your managers treat your people, what trust do you have in the service they are providing to your customers?

Where an organization has defined their approach, for example to wellbeing and benefits, this can be completely derailed by a poor or ineffective manager. The impact of a bad manager can result in lost time, poor customer service and a financial impact.

Look first at the capability of the managers within the organization. Have you determined what 'good' looks like? Is that broken down into the skills and behaviours you need your managers to have? And are those skills and behaviours clear and specific?

We want them to be commercial, lead strategy, performance manage their people, coach, instruct, deliver results, they need to understand the business, they need to be developing their people, they need to remove the poor performers, they need to shape the team, they need to be hands on, hands off, they need to be strategic, they need to be available, responsive to each and every email, they need to know what is happening in finite detail, they need a plan.

Wow. The role of any manager is all-encompassing, yet it is peppered with contradictions. Break down each part of the lifecycle of a manager and see which skills are prevalent and which skills and behaviours are shaping (consciously or not) the culture you have. For example, has it become acceptable for managers to not be part of the induction process? Do your managers have a meeting format they follow that is consistent across the business? Are they leading by example and being accountable for their actions? Are managers acting in a way that shows their teams that the ecosystem they are creating aligns with the overarching purpose and culture of the business?

When you have a great manager, performance increases, wellbeing is prevalent and costs are managed. For that reason, time must be spent in the culture design process considering how the leaders of the business can be aligned with the target culture.

If we look at the skills and behaviours that need to be demonstrated, they will differ by business and sector. If, for example, you are in the public sector, in a traditional hierarchical organization, then agile leadership is possibly not your thing. So, it needs to be congruent. If you are a digital marketing agency, no doubt you have creativity and innovation on the list. But what about the rest; what are the other attributes you want to see? Do you want them to be courageous or to play it safe? Do they have full autonomy or is it decision by committee? How do you want your teams to work together? If you are looking for a collaborative culture, are the managers and processes developed to make that happen? And who is writing these attributes?

Review the role. There will be managers who manage productivity, the number alone; due to the interchangeable nature of their agency workforce, they have no time to get to know the individual. The skills and behaviours of these managers will differ from the true people managers, those where it is more likely they have a permanent team. They know their people and they know their families. They have a deeper relationship, but they still have a responsibility to ensure that each of their team members is pulling in the same direction. Both are managers but review the detail of what is needed in each role.

Define the attributes that will execute the strategy and share them, internally and externally. They should be on all the job adverts. It should be what the resourcing team knows, as the bread and butter of the managers they are hiring.

I am not saying recruit robots who are all alike. You are looking for different skills, but just establish a baseline so people know this is the culture of the business. Where leaders lead in a similar way, it minimizes noise and reduces politics; agreement has already been made on the basics. If these are the themes agreed and executed by all the leaders in the business, then it results in the team being focused on the job and all distractions over what is fair and what's not are removed.

The golden thread of continuity is more than the values check, competencies check, job description check; it is about defining the culture you aspire to have, the strategic goals and the leadership style you need to thread it all together.

Feedback model: Stop, Start, Continue

Communication in the workplace shapes culture. If you are developing a culture where one of your values is along the lines of honesty or integrity or you are developing a learning culture, then an approach needs to be shaped for the process of giving and receiving feedback.

Feedback is an essential form of development. In any relationship, including director and apprentice or graduate mentoring programmes or reverse mentoring, a culture of feedback shows that all levels can continually learn and develop. Programmes such as these are not just for the benefit of the junior member but also for the benefit of the senior leader. If your senior leaders aren't connected to the generation of today and seeking to understand their world, they are limiting their thinking and the evolution of the culture. Diversity brings so much value to an organization; don't just have diversity – bring it to life.

The feedback model 'Stop, Start, Continue' is a clean method for achieving this. Straightforward, right! 'Great to see you in action; can I provide you with some feedback on what I have seen? I think you have shown real understanding of the task. How do you feel about doing this without seeking reassurance?... Start believing in your abilities. You are making all the right decisions, so continue doing this.'

That's feedback: it's honest, it's direct, there's no ambiguity and it's not a 'sh*t sandwich'. For those less familiar with this, the sh*t sandwich consists of Good, Bad and then the Good again! Having seen and experienced this in action over the years, I can confirm it results in one of two things.

1. The recipient has only heard the 'good' statement. Obvious, right, you told them twice and by putting in the 'developmental feedback' – which is what you should be focusing on – in the middle, you have completely lost impact.
2. The recipient is a 'dweller' – you know the sort; we have all met them and you may be one yourself. They have just received the highest of high praises... but it still won't be good enough. They seek perfection and what comes with this is a barrel-load of inner monologue, so give them a sh*t sandwich and they will

focus only on the 'sh*t'. It's particularly ineffective for this brood as you are not telling them what they need to do to improve.

Organizations with strong cultures use 'developmental feedback', which is simply what it states: feedback to help your development. It's purely about providing you with a specific area where you can improve and guidance on how you take the steps to achieve that improvement.

When we recognize that we each have a responsibility to develop those around us then feedback doesn't feel as threatening; it's merely a tool, an intervention that's there to help someone grow from good to great.

If this is a culture you seek, then induct everyone into your business in the feedback culture. Share how feedback can be provided from all directions. Share that the purpose is solely on improving what you did or how you could increase the impact. It's an acknowledgement that we all have blind spots, and we need each other to be able to help us reach the next level by removing the blind spots for us. When there is no ego and you have a culture where everyone's development interests are at the heart of it, then you will see teams working together and lifting each other up.

Further develop your managers in their observational skills. Managers with high emotional intelligence understand that their primary role is to understand their people, and to then understand how to get the best out of them. They will observe their team, they will see the smallest inflections or changes in behaviour, a flicker of emotion and, in a way they see suitable and at a time that's right, they will address this. They will ask the employee if they are OK; that might be enough and if not they might talk about what they have noticed and they will support the employee. Managers who get this will naturally have a high-performing team; their team will know they have someone who notices them – notices them as a person and supports them, whether it's work or a personal matter. And their intent to help was because they cared. Right there, that manager has created loyalty.

When it comes to management or leadership capability, don't just define what you want; remember to ask your employees, your colleagues. We have a new wave coming through, a generation who want development, they want progression, they want a coach to support them in their ongoing learning. If time pressures come under scrutiny and the leaders step into a command-and-control style, then they will squash what are the basic necessities of the employee. This generation is more demanding of the manager's time; they expect more, and they will leave the organization if their needs are not fulfilled. In your target culture design, consider that the world is changing, the needs of a new generation are different and the output needs to be an education to all whom it impacts.

Management and leadership development

We have already established that being a manager or leader is a key role. You are responsible for directing a group of people to fulfil a need. You have to create purpose, articulate the purpose, tell the story of what you are trying to achieve to engage your team and motivate them continually to deliver. And to manage the curveballs: priorities changing, team re-engagement and landing critical messages.

We live in a VUCA (Volatile, Uncertain, Complex and Ambiguous) world. We are dominated by change so naturally this seeps into the business world. While you are considering the skills your managers and leaders require, check whether they are equipped to handle change too. Do your managers have the skills to rise to this or are they fuelled by frustration? If you have managers who follow instruction and then lead by saying: 'Don't ask me why; the big cheese told me to, so just do it,' or worse, they slander the decisions, they are now slowly destroying the team they once had. The one that was so purposefully built they are subconsciously pulling down.

What level of importance do you put on your managers and leaders to lead change, to be resilient to the evolving world and to lead the team accordingly? Change is here to stay. How do your leaders create the followship required? How does this fit with the culture you want?

Once you know the culture you aspire to then part of your plan will be based on educating your people. Review your existing 'management development programme'. And consider whether you have a programme that meets the needs of the culture you are trying to shape. Who goes on it? Has it been designed so it is mandatory that every new manager joining the business attends or is it voluntary? What is your stance on this? If you want to set expectations from the off, then you need to ensure that what is being communicated is impacting all employees in your organization and not just the managers who seek out personal development.

Whether you have a programme (a series of modules), career pathway, online learning combining all the aforementioned or a toolkit (electronic or not), the question is, how do you check for understanding and application of learning? Not completion – completion rates are irrelevant; it is application that you are looking for. Does the seasoned manager, who joined with ten years' leadership experience, understand how you do things within your business? Educating seasoned managers isn't about discrediting their skills and behaviours. You are simply aligning them with how you do things in your business.

Two considerations:

1. *New first-time managers*: What support is provided for them to move into their first managerial role? Do they know what is now expected of them; are the development interventions planned and timely? Are the development interventions designed in accordance with the culture? Are they too much, too

little? Is the new manager provided with support, a mentor, a coach? What manager check-ins are they getting? And if they are an internal hire, what additional development is provided which allows them to take that step from peer to manager? And who is checking the consistent application of learning in the workplace?

2. *New managers to the business*: What are the development interventions being scheduled in? Are they the right interventions to support the understanding of the culture? Have you sheep-dipped or have you completed a gap analysis? Is it mandatory or voluntary? Do they know what is expected of them? And what support is provided to ensure they are getting it right?

Management development is crucial and should be prevalent in all businesses, large or small. The natural-born leaders in school will thrive with the right education; the less natural leaders will develop with the right support and conditions.

But there are so many variations of management development: some learn through highly esteemed programmes, some learn from reading and e-learning and others through on-the-job learning. For your business, ensure a line is placed in the sand and you have a benchmark of what is acceptable. Educate your managers from the minute they first engage with you. Lay out expectations and ask them what support they need to get there, the areas of development they think they need more of. Showcase the feedback model, be open, and explain why the ongoing development of the managers' skills in line with your culture is so important to you as a business. If you have done the recruitment right, then chances are you already have a leader with a growth mindset who understands; this isn't teaching them to sucks eggs but is about leading a culture in your business.

Developing the rest of the business

And then there is the rest of the business. What development opportunities are provided for all employees to grow? Is your target culture one where growth is key and if not, why not? A business that doesn't adopt a growth mindset is one that will stagnate quickly. Productivity will be impacted by lack of skill to accomplish the job, competence will dip and employees will be left feeling uninvested.

In a business where development is an afterthought, this permeates into all aspects. For example, a team's delivery plan isn't always used to its full capacity. The manager can see what skills are required in each project and yet fails to acknowledge what they need in advance. The questions to the team 'Do we have the skills in the team? And are they available at point of need for this project?' are often missed and with that the opportunity lost to develop the skills of one of the team or an advance approach to someone from outside of the team to fulfil the need. The lack of foresight and practical action results in unnecessary pressure being applied on everyone.

Where there are learning cultures, development means something to the businesses, the investment in employees' development is active, and the employees feel valued. Development is more than a 'training session'; it's the feedback provided, the development built into team meetings; it's the accountability of learning that is owned by each employee and encouraged by each manager. The results are seen in the behaviours: curiosity spiked, questions asked, health challenges minimized and an environment of psychological safety.

Developing your approach to learning and development stems from knowing the culture you want to have. These questions should be asked:

- Who can access development?
- What development can they access?

- Is time provided for everyone to develop?
- Who owns development (a team, the manager or each individual)? If you keep getting a low score on your employee opinion survey on the question 'Does the company invest in your development?' then look at the culture. Have you sent them on one course this year and that's all the 'training' they have received?
- How effective is the learning provided then applied?
- Do you push development or are your employees pulling it?
- Is the learning that's on offer what the employee wants/needs?
- What value do your senior leaders put on learning?

Are the answers to the questions aligned with your target culture?

The learning and development function should understand the capability of the employees from within the business, the gaps in capability (skills and behaviours) and what investment is required to bridge that gap. Whether or not new behaviours are adopted or ignored needs to be continually monitored. It needs to be more than 'Level 1 analysis – happy sheets' filled in with responses such as 'Yeah, I'm happy to have a day off to attend something where I got a great feed.' This output needs to be much more. You can use attendance/non-attendance rates, as this will inform you of what the culture is like; are people too important to attend development sessions? Or are they not allowed out of the business because there is no flex in the organization? Or can everyone access the development they need, when and how they want it?

When we look at the success of the application of learning, it's important to look at the 'four levels of competence'. This was described first by Martin Broadwell as the 'four levels of teaching' in 1969.[4] The four levels of competence describe the psychology behind each stage we go through when we progress from incompetence to competence – a stage of complete unknowing to being fully competent.

The easiest example is 'learning how to drive a car'. You are 16 going on 30 and think, 'Driving is easy, I'll smash this, a couple of lessons and I'll pass! No bother.' This is Stage 1, 'Unconsciously Incompetent', which essentially means you are at a stage where you have no idea about how little you know about that topic.

Next you pick up your theory test book, which you need to revise. You immediately become overwhelmed by the size of it, the markings, the signs and all these laws you now need to learn. You're already exclaiming that it is too much to learn, and this is then coupled with getting into the car and being shown a host of buttons. You have now reached the next stage, 'Consciously Incompetent'. You now are fully aware of the skills you need but are still incompetent.

A number of lessons later, you are revising and it feels like you understand the practicalities of both the practical and the theory. This is 'Conscious Competence'; you know what you need to do but it requires effort and concentration.

Lastly, fast-forward six months: test passed, bad habits formed, you have reached 'Unconscious Competence'. What took so long to learn now doesn't even require thinking about. You know how to drive a car; everything you have learnt now simply happens.

---

[4] M. M. Broadwell, 'Teaching for learning (XVI.)', *The Gospel Guardian*, 20(41) (1969), 1–3. Available from www.wordsfitlyspoken.org/gospel_guardian/v20/v20n41p2_image.html [accessed 8 January 2021].

Business with risk

It is also pertinent to point out that if you have employees who have a job that has risk, then conscious competence is the place to be. We have all driven a route one day, arrived at the destination and can't remember the drive. You worked on autopilot; this is where accidents can happen. If your employees' safety is paramount to the culture you are trying to create, then when you're developing the training for those particular tasks you need to have considered how to keep reinforcing the learning, keeping the employees' mindset in Stage 3, Consciously Competent.

The reason I have included this is that any cultural development programme is going to have a change impact. To deliver change into a business, it will need to have a development programme shaped to achieve it. The programme should be designed to develop the behaviours within your employees that will move you towards your target culture. It brings awareness to people of what the new culture looks like, what the required skills are, building a safety net for trial and error and showing that failure is welcomed without reprimand, until conscious competence is achieved and then ultimately the shift to unconscious competence. But remember, that's not it; ongoing nurturing should still continue or behaviours can slip.

Review the learning and development strategy, its alignment to the business plan and to the culture you are developing. Where businesses build learning interventions with continuity, the cultural theme threads through each interaction. The leadership programme has the cultural needs shaped and embedded into it. Career planning, digital learning, coaching, and team development are all aligned with the aspirational culture. The learning and development team knows where you are headed and the organizational development will be built to future-proof you and the leaders.

Coaching culture

If you have decided to go one step further and are working towards a coaching culture then, again, all development and processes need to be considered. There needs to be acknowledgement that this takes time, particularly if it involves a transformation of your existing culture.

In a business where a coaching culture is prevalent, the managers/leaders are developed as competent coaches. This creates an environment of trust and creates psychological safety, which in turn creates a space for innovation. The managers/coaches remove the limiting beliefs in others, they uncover a person's potential, they motivate employees, and their self-belief grows. Hierarchy is sidelined in favour of partnership and collaboration.

The organization's success is typically a by-product. The service that leaders provide changes the dynamic. They no longer get what they historically asked for; they get more. Success/targets/performance, all that was expected was achieved because their people gave more. Quality, accountability, innovation are more prevalent – innovation that's put into action, generating better outcomes. Outcomes they may never have known existed. The opportunities are exponential.

Talent development

What is 'talent' within your business? Some organizations call everyone talent; it doesn't matter whether you're the CEO or the cleaner, you are talent as you have a purpose that contributes to the overall success of the business. Then there are others that see talent as their top performers, or those that they have identified as having the potential to move into senior roles.

Talent and the process around talent management can be contentious so we need to look at this to see how it impacts the culture of your organization. How qualified are the managers or leaders in identifying talent? What support do you give managers in understanding the full talent management process?

If you are in a large organization, does the 9 box grid work for you?[5] Is it fair; how much time are your managers spending talking about which box is the most suitable box versus the development that is needed? When you are calibrating, does it work? The leader who has just character assassinated one of their own; who is challenging them? Surely this is a self-declaration that you are not fulfilling your role as coach/educator? Development is the responsibility of the manager so if they are not performing then neither are you. This is your chance to show they aren't where they need to be, but you know how to get them there.

Identify your talent, but know what talent is, what you're looking for. Know the skills, behaviours and attributes you need to drive the culture forward. Those who crave development and want to progress for the benefit of the wider team and the business.

And where potential leaders of tomorrow are identified, then review the development solutions (training, online learning, coaching, mentoring); review that they are not replicas of talent programmes in the industry but are about the leaders of tomorrow in your business aligned with your culture. Create space for talent to think, provide tools that can be used, create a space for trial and error and provide business projects that allow for growth. Safely stretch talent and create a ground swell, a network who collaborate, who feel each corner of the business through their experience and their network.

---

[5] AIHR Analytics, 'The 9 box grid: A practitioner's guide'. Available from www.analyticsinhr.com/blog/9-box-grid [accessed 18 January 2021].

Employee relations/policies and processes

Now I'll be honest, this isn't my area of expertise, nor have I ever been pulled into this arena, whether it be for my career or where I have had to manage someone's performance formally within my own team. I always wondered if, for a manager who always has employee relations cases on the go, whether this is reflective of their industry, their business, or whether this is an indicator of their own ability as a manager?

I appreciate that managing people is not always easy; it comes with a high degree of complexity. Managing a function is one thing, a budget another, performance targets attainable, but managing the ins and outs of people's behaviour requires emotional intelligence.

When you are in the process of data gathering, you should have identified the volume of disciplinaries, grievances and tribunals. Do you have a high volume? Is this down to behaviour or a new manager coming in who is performance managing accordingly? Or is it a low number, due to behaviour or performance avoidance? What did your data indicate? What have you learnt in comparing the data across the business? What do your findings say about your culture or ecosystems of culture within sub-teams?

In businesses where there is a culture of avoidance there is a turning of a blind eye. You can see this not just in the inaction of managers but also in the language they use, particularly when talking about poor performers, language like 'conflict'. When challenged 'Is it really conflict?' you uncover that it is typically the paradigm of the managers, a legacy culture of 'it would be too much hassle to deal with'. So a shift is required, a change of language to position that this is a conversation based on evidence that requires a conversation. It's not contentious; there should be no bias. Managers act on basic assumptions. Could that be capability, could it be lack of support, or is that a culture that has developed where managers are doing what they think is right?

Next, look at your people policies and at what they are saying is and isn't acceptable. Are they detailed or are they vague? If detailed, how are you ensuring that your managers understand the detail of the policies and then how and when should they enforce the action that surrounds them?

If they are vague, have they been written in a style that implies what the policy should mean without the detail? How are you landing this with your managers? What is deemed acceptable and what's not?

It may be that you are in a business where your managers are setting and managing expectations and so employee relations cases are minimal. The culture is one where communication is key and is demonstrated in the team's effectiveness. Clear expectations are set, performance is continually managed and active challenge is the norm. There is the continued pursuit of team development to deliver the results for the business... Ongoing development right there.

Those are the businesses that are challenging how the policies should be written. Moving towards an adult-to-adult (transactional analysis) policy, this works in organizations that have matured the capability of their employees in line with a culture of accountability.

Your managers are employed to manage. They need to be given the direction about how you want them to manage in line with the culture you are trying to create: what's acceptable, what's not, how they deal with things that aren't, how they manage the wider impact of the team. This way they remain people and performance focused simultaneously.

Environment

'Cultural architect' would be a great job title; it shouts experiential. If we look at a business that maximizes the 'experience' then we only have to look as far as Apple. From the stores, the help, the technology, but best of all, and this is because I'm a marketer's dream, the packaging. The packaging is on another level... no stone unturned, their products built and designed for the user. So knowing what we know, do you think the environment the employees work in would be any different? Absolutely not, they value high quality and to realize that effectively doesn't mean housing employees in a bleak, 1970s-reminiscent grey office. No, they have created an environment that allows the thinkers to think, innovators to innovate, and so on. They understood their needs and they met them. Apple knew who they wanted to be.

In organizations where there is cultural alignment with who you want to be, the environment, or as Schein put it, 'the artefacts', maximizes the potential of the people it accommodates.

In cultures where this is not the case, the mere thought of 'going into the office' is met with a morose feeling. I once worked with an organization where the culture was deep rooted. It was toxic; people felt undervalued, unappreciated, and were unconnected to the business and its purpose. When the management took time to listen to the team's woes, they chose only to hear the complaints about the physical environment, so the action taken was to redecorate. They literally 'painted over the cracks'.

The environment should be conducive to the culture you are trying to create. If you are looking to create an environment that allows free thinking, for idea generation and collaboration, is the working environment set up with this at the heart of its design? If it's a high-productivity business, have you created a lean environment?

When the environment is conducive to the culture it is authentic. For example, if you are a red-tape-laden, bureaucratic organization steeped in hierarchy then it's likely you'll have a traditional corporate environment: board rooms, meeting rooms, less open space, meeting rooms named accordingly. It mirrors the culture of the business and it works.

If you are in tech or a business thriving with entrepreneurial thinkers then we have seen the development of cool,
funky, lofty premises. These are designed to attract the generation that is progressive in their style and ambition and the
environment is designed in congruence with this.

When looking at culture, take time to see if the environment reflects what you are trying to achieve; it has to be right
for your business. Start with making sure the basics are there.
If the basic fundamentals aren't there, then don't question
why your employees aren't respecting the workplace.

Take your time to review where you are spending the
money of the business. How much of it is to ensure the environment is designed to get the best from your people? Do
you offer free vending machine services? Or do you have a
barista on each floor serving almond milk lattes? How are
your employees welcomed each morning? And each evening,
what is it like leaving? In one business, employees were faced
with gridlock when leaving each night; the business identified the problem and staggered departure time. This met the
needs of the business and the employees, and engagement
naturally increased. People like to be listened to and when
that results in action it makes their lives a little easier; in turn,
watch the employees give back. In your review, engage with
your employees; ask how you can support your employees to
eliminate some of life's frustrations. Opening the conversation will pay dividends in building your target culture.

Blatantly obvious, I hear you say... but unfortunately,
the above points are not always actioned. If you walk into
your business tomorrow with fresh eyes, the eyes of a new
employee, what does it feel like? What do you notice that you
had become blind to? What are the frustrations impacting the
day that need resolving and is there someone there listening
and taking action? Even when the budget is limited, there
are always things that can be done that show you are listening
and acting in the interests of your people.

When acting on your research, change of environment along with any change is best served when the teams impacted in that space are fully engaged with. Don't have an office refit and declare it a total success when the reality to the employee is 'it's a total disaster'. Things like the open-plan, trendy new office allowing no space for difficult conversations. Or the overhead lighting being headache inducing. Make sure you have asked what people want and then ask if what you do meets their needs. Does it work for them?

Remote working

When the Covid-19 pandemic impacted the world in 2020, droves of employees were tasked to work from home, while home-schooling children where necessary. With culture in mind, there was a clear shift; there were environmental impacts that meant the workforce became disparate. How did you equip your people to adapt to the physical environment change? What working parameters did you put in place? Did they get the kit that met their needs, the tech and the infrastructure to keep them connected with the business and its purpose? And if you had a collaborative working culture, how did you deal with the environmental change?

Were you able to equip your teams with not just the technical but also the emotional new way of working? Were you able to assist your employees in the shift of mindset involved in moving from an environment where human interaction was commonplace to the removal of all face-to-face stimuli?

Organizations that considered the impact on the person, the productivity impact, reforecasting deliverables in line with the physical changes were able to support their people in a way that kept their teams working together despite being physically apart. Wellbeing factored in, they were the companies who continued to perform.

Do not lose sight of how you maintain the momentum of a new employee in both office and remote aspects. Where people have a clear purpose that's aligned to the values and the business, their motivation will be high, but you have to maintain that. This comes only with ensuring the environment provides them with the stimulus and connection for them to feel the impact of their role.

With the world continually evolving, technological advancement has led to the new remote worker. How will you create a future-facing environment that continues to evolve? How much time do you spend considering the impact of the environment on your employees and the culture that creates?

Communication

If we were to strip back to the basics of communication, its purpose is to impart and receive information. Of equal importance are the messages you wish to send out and the reception and interpretation of the messages. Basic, but sometimes the latter is overlooked.

Communication and engagement (if you formally have both) are responsible for helping all employees join the dots; they need to lift the strategy of the organization, link it to the vision and the culture and curate content that continually pulls the golden thread through.

The team members are responsible for the continual review of all the communication channels to see what is and isn't working and then to amend accordingly. They need knowledge of the mix of the employees, how people like to be communicated with, not just the channels, but the method, the style, who they like hearing the messages from. This is a big factor in large organizations, where corporate messaging can feel hugely disconnected and irrelevant to those 'on the ground'. So how do they bridge that gap and make the communications meaningful?

In organizations with a weak culture, communication can be ineffective, and vice versa. In organizations with weak communication, the culture can also be fragmented. These are the organizations that fail to check to see if the receivers of the communication understood the message and took the call to action. A disproportionate amount of time is spent on pushing communications out compared with time spent understanding the employees, their needs and whether what they are sending lands in the way it was intended.

Organizations with strong cultures are aware and maximize the use of their communications and the many forms of communicating. The strategy of the teams is to ensure that the right messaging is going out to the right people, in the right way, and that it is steeped in the cultural narrative of the organization. The owners of the communications are fully aware that they are the gatekeepers, that they are responsible for what should and shouldn't be going out, managing communications in a timely manner and always ensuring that the message is on point. With each communication that is shaped, they ask a preliminary question: 'What is the emotion this communication should invoke? Is it positivity, is it encouragement, celebration, empathy?' They follow this up with: 'What is the intention of the communication?' Communications without this consideration are already diluted and missing the impact and opportunity to further strengthen the organizational culture.

There are also organizations who are building a culture where wellbeing is a key factor. They have seen the impact of communication overload and have taken steps to relieve the stress this placed on their employees. These are the businesses trialling initiatives such as the following:

No email day: The one day a week where everyone speaks to each other, phone dependent, or you walk through the office or the warehouse to see who you need to contact!

Organizations that have done this reaped the benefits: relations improved, productivity improved, they had time in the week to focus on getting work done without it being interspersed with the constant pinging of emails. A number of businesses saw a drop in emails over the rest of the working week; people began speaking to each other more. The result was increased productivity: one interaction meant the question was answered and the problem resolved. This was instead of a thread of emails that never really got to the correct resolution.

No emails post 4pm (unless business critical): I can already hear the backlash to this monstrosity of an idea. The heckles of 'but it's in the evening that I get back on top of my work,' 'I have to as I can't start the day already flooded with emails.' Listen to what you are saying. Is your organization one that has wellbeing at its core or is your organization one that has driven a behaviour that disregards time for self? If you knew that no emails were coming into your inbox from 4pm, or OK, 5pm onwards, how would that make you feel? How productive would your last hour of the working day be, so you could clear your emails knowing that you can go home to an uninterrupted evening with zero pings? Would this be a benefit that you would savour more than 20% off a gym membership?

No emails at all: All communications are on public boards; it minimizes traffic but means that everyone in the business has full visibility of what is going on and the decisions being made. It ensures that people are picking up the phone to talk to their colleagues. Decisions are made faster because everyone is present. Then they update on the communal board. Consider the impact that has on the team's decision making. If every decision was made public, would the decision makers be more considerate to the wider impact of their decisions? Would their thinking naturally be broadened because the minute it is out in the ether, then any other team impacted would immediately have their say, therefore the decision they make has to be for the overall good of the business? It removes teams making key decisions that are only for the benefit or for the ease of themselves.

What would work for you from the above? As a nation, presenteeism is a workplace culture: 'Yes, I was logged on till 11pm last night trying to get on top of my workload,' 'Ouch, my inbox is sitting at 300 unread emails and I only stepped away from my laptop for a millisecond.' How does this align with who you want to be? If this culture resonates within your business, then ask yourself why? Why are people feeling like they need to share how busy they are? Or that they feel the need to wear their demand as a badge of honour? Or are your employees unequivocally overwhelmed with what's expected of them and inadvertently asking for help?

Cultures where accountability is key see an overwhelming reduction in emails... Bliss! For emails where line managers are copied in – as god forbid, someone has just agreed to something, but just in case it was a wrong decision people cover themselves – the volume falls away.

In organizations where we employ adults to do a job, where there is accountability and psychological safety, the need to have to copy someone else in disappears. The feeling of security within the business has a much greater value on performance.

Be honest in your review. Has your business become a slave to email; is the primary communication method one in line with the target culture, or do you need a reset? Look at the behaviours you see – are they productive or damaging? This is not just the volume of emails, or the line manager being copied in, but the behaviours where every man and his dog is on an email thread. A mistake has been made and then the repercussion that reverberates around your internal system is the virtual placing of the mistake into virtual blocks and virtual shaming with virtual tomatoes, virtual cabbage and a touch of virtual defecation all launched at their virtual face... For all to see! Hurrah, what a tirade, made by someone who has the power of the keyboard. The infamous person who does not have the guts to say it to your face but behind a keyboard instead. How proud they must be of those powerful shaming digits of theirs.

If this occurs in your business; stop it. Stop the public shaming and educate employees in the development of communication and impact. Ask them what culture they are creating by doing what they are doing and if this is really who they want to be? Make them see: this is monstrous to any form of culture. This is damaging your employees; they are slowly being chipped away at and will soon let you know when they have had enough.

Review your communication process and decide what is acceptable and what is not.

- What is the volume of emails sent across the business a day? (Gather data from IT. What is the volume of email traffic, peaks and troughs?)
- What percentage of them are required?
- What practice do you have in place for when people go on holiday? How about an email block? The world is moving so fast; emails are soon out of date.
- Are the communications sent out effective? Too many, too few?
- What culture is created by the processes you have in place?

Do you have a team responsible for communications that reports on the culture of the communication within the business? Not just what they push out. Are they monitoring what the communication culture has become and strategizing what it should be like? And are they proposing to the board to challenge when the culture has fallen out of sync with the cultural aspiration?

Using tech to communicate

Love it or loathe it, the intranet in medium and large organizations is still commonplace and in some is used as the only way to communicate with employees. But seriously, who has the time? Who sits there scouring the intranet for the latest tidbit?

If you have an intranet, organizations who haven't wrapped their arms around it don't know how many hits the site and its pages are getting. The content is misaligned with the culture and further shared accountability of the site by business area further creates inconsistency. Neglected efforts result in the pages being dormant or out of date.

But where businesses have got this right, the communication team either owns the site in its entirety, or is working with the business, coaching the 'tone of voice', in line with the culture. They are partnering and educating to build their content, to showcase their teams and the information they want to share. They labour the importance of communication, embedding a two-way process in line with the culture of the organization. Review the data at hand to understand what is being achieved.

- Look at the detail at a granular level; what are people reading?
- How many reactions (emoticons) are being given by the readers to the articles/posts a day?
- When were your employees last asked what would they like to read about?
- How do your employees like to receive your communications? How about audible comms? Videos?
- Where are the communications coming from? Are they all corporate communications, or have you handed communications over to the employees, or a balance?

There are organizations that understand that 50% of their workforce are millennials, growing to a predicted number of 75% by 2025. They are reviewing and designing methods of communications that fit the demographics of the business. With a generation of Instagram stories, reels, tweets and TikTok, consider a 'people culture', one that allows 'the people' to own their own communications. Yes, put some governance in, but allow them to video their teams, themselves, the project they are landing, the big deals they have won, the infrastructure they are providing. The ingenuity of style and the freedom for communication will be out there. People will take pride in it. They will create new ways of landing their message in the best possible way. Yes, provide them with guidelines to work with but allow them the freedom to create. It goes back to what do you want the culture to be and how are the team's strategies directed to meet that cause? As a receiver of this style of information, this creativity is so much more impactful.

Could this have more impact than senior leaders who have been sitting in the same staged office positioned next to some strategically placed greenery to bring colour to what can typically be a lacklustre performance? Or where senior leaders present an egomaniacal video that isn't culturally aligned or a launch video of something that should be fever pitch but comes across monotone? These are the thoughts and challenges that need to come from the communications team. It is their responsibility to affect the quality and impact of communication in the business.

Now we know that not all senior leaders can stand in front of an audience in person or appear on video comfortably, and that's OK. But the team filming need to be able to be honest. Create a plan; how can you best get them to land their messages in a way that meets the purpose in a kind way?

Communications is the team that has the responsibility from the outset of the cultural design – to hold a mirror to the organization; not any old mirror, a full-length, golden, ornate, Snow White 'Mirror, mirror on the wall' mirror. They need to know that their role is to stand on the other side of the mirror. They are integral to the credibility of the organization and the culture that is communicated. Honest feedback about who should appear in the company's internal and external communications is key.

Yes leaders, be the figurehead but allow the employees who have passionately delivered to showcase their results. It will be authentic; it screams a culture of inclusivity, collaboration, creativity, and above all else, accountability. People will own it.

The receivers of the information will learn more about the teams, about the individuals they have seen. They have the opportunity now to stop them in the corridor and say: 'Loved your video; what a project! That must have been a great opportunity.' The unknown becomes the known, relationships are built, networking aids development, which aids opportunity. You are opening doors.

Allow (within regulations) the upload of such videos to social media, even the outtakes, and who doesn't love an outtake? That moment where you're doubled up with tears streaming down your face and bubbles of excitement are escaping, when you're trying your upmost best to be serious. The team being completely real with each other, stripped of the *idea of professionalism* and flooded with raw laughter. You have your employees selling your business to prospective clients and to prospective employees. It's real, it's fun, its engaging... being your real self is allowed and celebrated.

I digress, but communications – the methods, the process – help define a culture. The communications team are the gatekeepers to cultural alignment and their role is critical in the cultural narrative. Everything they communicate must tell the story of who the business is and how every communications update fits with the purpose, the values and behaviours of how it has been achieved.

Develop your cultural narrative and allow the team to work with the business to build this into every interaction and every communication. Work with them to assess the quality and impact of each communication and measure the shift in culture, based on the unity of message. Give the team the opportunity to confront, to challenge; it's for the greater good of the business and will create a groundswell of positive action. Make sure your IT function is there at the front providing innovation solutions to the communication challenges you may face. This is an example where teams need to work internally to create the right solutions for the business. The communication strategy cannot be looked at in silos. The key strategies that need to be brought together are the communications strategy, the business strategy, the leadership development strategy and the cultural ambition. These are the threads that when entwined with each other accelerate you to the culture you desire.

Engagement

Engagement in many medium to large organizations typically forms part of the communications team. This is not about understanding a message – that still should sit in the communication remit. Engagement is so much more and therefore needs a strategy on its own.

It can have a huge impact on culture and on the bottom line. According to a 2016 Gallup study, the business units in the top quartile of Gallup's employee engagement database are 17% more productive and 21% more profitable than those in the bottom quartile.[6]

The role and purpose of engagement has a serious financial number attached to it. Yet it is not always given the attention it deserves. If your productivity is low, if your numbers aren't met, or projects are not landing on time, look beyond the excuses. What is the culture like and how engaged are your employees with it?

Imagine you have been told an election is due to take place; you understand your choices and you can vote. Does that mean you are engaged? Not necessarily, not if the options

---

[6] Gallup, 'Do employees really know what's expected of them?' 27 September 2016. Available from https://news.gallup.com/business-journal/195803/employees-really-know-expected.aspx [accessed 18 January 2021].

you have been provided with don't meet your needs and your selection is purely one of indifference.

To be engaged organizationally, there needs to be buy-in. 'I have chosen this as the place I want to come to every day, and I like my choice. I'm not ready to go anywhere; I would recommend this as a great place to work and actively encourage others to join.' This is interesting considering that, unlike the election, the organization is not democratic. You did not vote in the leader or the leader's leader. Similarly, they may or may not have chosen you to join their team; you may have been inherited. So mutual engagement needs to take place.

Engagement is so much more than the 'annual employee survey'. It is a constant thread in the organization. Ignoring issues will result in disengagement, which results in politics, lost time and ultimately lost bottom line. To reiterate, engagement can make the business 21% more profitable. Organizations that recognize this reap the rewards.

So, who owns engagement? Simply put, everyone. If you have a team responsible for engagement, then they should be the driving force in continually pulling together the golden thread. They need to be mapping the engagement points to ensure that the tapestry of strategy, vision, mission, business updates and the culture are interwoven into everything they create. Be sure to challenge misalignment or engagement will dip. Are they identifying when a particular team or even the manager has become disengaged and how are they addressing it? This is a proactive and a preventative function; this is bottom-line impact. So just how high on the agenda is it? They should have the analytics and be able to explain why this has happened and what needs to be done to recover it.

They are the doorway in and out of communications; their ears should be on the ground. They need to know what is going on, what's next and how the employees feel about what is happening. The employee opinion surveys, the forums, the conferences; they are all staples of engagement. What is the story, how compelling is it, are your employees listening and receptive to it, or do they need something else? You also have your leaders and managers who also own engagement. What interventions do they have to increase their engagement? How are learning and development developing the skills in the business? Do you employ leaders with these skills, or for their technical ability?

Leaders who understand culture and understand engagement provide clear direction. They are the coxswain of a rowing team. They have created an environment that allows freedom for thinking, freedom for challenge, a team that accelerates further and faster than any Oxbridge team because they own this. This is one engaged team; they don't need to be told, as they are a step ahead. The engagement has created a team of people who want the organization, your organization, to thrive and the thrill of it is that they are here, right beside you. Not behind; beside you. You cannot afford for one member of your team to start rowing in the opposite direction as chances are that they will start taking the others with them and that's when culture is impacted.

In smaller businesses, you are naturally closer to your people and may be reliant on instinct to tell you whether or not your team is engaged. I am a believer in instinct, but I am also of the opinion that when the person responsible for great instinct is distracted with business-critical activity, when the pressure is on, then instinct is dialled down or ignored. It becomes a problem area that you don't have time to deal with until it's too late. Don't be reliant on empathy: 'Can't they see I'm up to my neck in this? I don't have time for it.' Your problems are not their problems.

Make time for engagement: your employees matter; they are an asset that like your physical assets will depreciate in value if you don't tend to them.

Communication and engagement are everywhere: physically in the environment, in the spoken and non-spoken word. By being clear in your efforts it will give you the outputs you need. This is the very essence of every part of the thread that binds us.

Meetings

Meetings are a cultural indicator of the business. Many a judgement is made by a visitor on the culture of the organization from attending a meeting.

Now I am the kind of person who rocks up; I'm there, face to face or virtually, I am there. And by saying 'I'm there', I really mean I am there, I am fully in the moment, I am present. I will have brought pre-work if necessary, I will have done my actions, any queries that I may have needed to have had offline, I would have taken offline and discussed separately.

But this is not always the case in some cultures. Instead, the voluminous meetings are imposed, each with the cast of Ben-Hur in attendance. There's a lack of focus due to ineffective chairing of the meeting and a lack of structure.

There are expectations of consistent energy and focus required for an all-day meeting despite the rising stress levels gained by those who had to be taken away from their day job. Or worse still, they are simultaneously trying to be there and do the day job and yet this is still ignored. You have just halved their effectiveness in both the meeting and their day job. Are your expectations too high?

My tolerance of poorly executed meetings has definitely waned over time. Too many meetings happen for meetings' sake; decision by committee as no one wants to take accountability. Meetings are rescheduled due to lack of attendance. Relationships are strained as it's always the same people not having provided an update or completed their actions as they were tasked, resulting in a repetition of last week. And then they are not challenged.

Simply put, meetings are not, nor should they be, used as a circus ground. They should be the coming together of a group of necessary people to make a decision, to collaborate, to generate ideas, to update.

Only the people who need to be there should be there, and those who are there need to be present. Turn up on time, be there mind, body and soul, contribute and if you have actions, do them. The way meetings are executed highlights the culture in many ways. Are the attendees there on time, do they see the importance and their role in the meeting, are they putting things into action and moving them forward? Or are they late, inattentive, removed from any accountability or, worse, so full of their own self-importance that they use the meeting to put on their latest rendition of me, myself and I?

For non-attendance, follow up with why? Why is it acceptable to not show up? To not send a message about what unavoidable thing was prioritized? If people can't attend meetings nor send an apology to their own peers, what level of service are they providing to your customers?

Consider the principles you have in your business around meetings. What meetings have to be face to face; what can be done virtually? What is acceptable and what is not? Do you have a culture where you have people on conference calls who are using that time to write up the last meeting's actions, emailing, doing expenses or handling other calls that come through? If they are not needed, why are they on the call? Being 'on a call' is not offering their name at the beginning of the call so it appears they are in a meeting, when realistically they weren't present. Are you maximizing people's time or is time a commodity being wasted?

Organizations that manage their meetings and the time of their people are open and transparent about their meeting culture. Where they need someone to join a meeting to make a small contribution, they contribute beforehand or they join for their segment. Give people choices that drive a higher level of commitment.

They also develop their managers to manage the meetings with impact. Meetings have a defined purpose and structure, with effective messaging and handling of delegates. They lead conference calls where they have a list of the attendees' names and use the list to ask for contributions from all attendees throughout the meeting. They keep everyone engaged as they have already established that those who need to be there have a purpose.

Consider the following factors:

Cost up the average cost of people's time for a typical one-hour meeting in your business. Are you getting the maximum contribution, value and output for the investment you are putting in? If not, think differently about how you are using your people's time.

Rate your meetings. Why not? Why when performance, targets and all other angles of the business are measured should we not measure the effectiveness of a meeting? This is one of the biggest time-killers in the workplace and they are never performance managed!

Duration – any meeting that is an all-day meeting will be challenging. Are your meetings conducive? Are all-day meetings down to the volume of things needing to be discussed or is it down to poor time management?

Senior leadership meeting – how are they perceived by the teams in the business? What gets cascaded down, if at all? Or is it managed effectively; the key decisions shared to the rest of the employees for inclusion?

Board – how do you check how you are perceived? How do you want to be perceived? What action do you collectively take to ensure that you are driving the culture you set out and not hindering it? What is perceived about your meetings by your teams?

Board impact

I find it fascinating to observe guests preparing themselves for a guest slot to present at a board or senior team meeting. This is a great indicator as to the culture you have. Are your guests fearful; are they apprehensive? Or are they open, excited? Do they feel like they can show up being their best self? Or are they waiting for their slot shaking in the corner like a dog with rabies?

There are still senior leaders who choose not to take the time to appreciate what someone of lesser seniority (ranking in said business) has to say. The prevalence of power and ego stops the leader from gaining something so valuable it could be an organizational game changer. Are your senior leaders hosting meetings that allow for ideas to be presented? How are they embracing ideas and challenge? Do they drive innovation through embracing their people or are they inadvertently stifling ideas, instilling fear and terrorizing the individual who has just stepped into the lion's cage dressed in Lady Gaga's steak dress?

The board, the senior team impact, determines the culture – the way they behave, the words that are said, the meetings along with the action or inaction that follows; they are the undercurrent that flows into each and every interaction. How the board behaves will determine how others behave, in and out of meetings. The board's image is seen and reflected back through your teams. If you are seeing behaviours that you don't like, then check that these aren't first created by someone in authority who by their own actions has made them acceptable.

If you want to be more effective, look at other businesses who have a culture of efficiency and effectiveness and look at what you can gain. These are the organizations that use online tools for support. There are also businesses who have implemented structure and behaviour such as:

Opening meetings – 'left luggage' is a really nice way of starting a meeting to get everyone to offload all their woes or celebrations onto post-it notes at the beginning of the session. This includes anything that is on their mind and could distract their attention.

And if the employee needs to sound off or share, they asterisk the post-it. The chairperson gives that individual the airtime to work through their particular issue. It's a cathartic way to offload or to allow a celebratory moment. Once this is done, the meeting formally starts and everyone's focus is on the subject at hand.

Closing meetings should never be neglected: summarize, run through the agreed actions, agree the dates for the actions, agree who will share the decisions and actions with any non-attendees. And then before you close consider a concept like *benefits and concerns*. Each member has a turn. Not only does everyone have the chance to share their opinion, but you find out whether the meeting was of benefit and what that benefit was. It may have struck a chord with someone that they now want to do something off the back of it. It gives you insights where you may not have got them had you not asked. You may find out that the meeting wasn't of benefit at all, in which case you can find out why. Maybe they shouldn't be in the room; if so, have an honest conversation about it and agree a way forward.

Then you get the concerns, a great way of getting those who haven't voiced their opinion through the course of the meeting to finally have their say. This could mean back-pedalling over some of the previous discussion points, but either way everyone feels listened to; they have contributed and left the meeting feeling heard and valued. So already the people who need to be involved are fully committed for the next meeting, should there be one.

Meetings are a flashing beacon of what the culture is. They highlight what is acceptable and what isn't from a business angle; they show people's behaviour, the level they contribute and the acceptance of accountability. They expose so much. Are people being valued? Are you really listening to your people or have bad behaviours seeped into the way you do things, and those behaviours are being ignored? This will eventually seep into your meetings with external suppliers and customers; it is your organizational brand and identity you are damaging if you have got this wrong. Review your meetings; they are the windows to the soul of a business.

Time to leave

You've been with your other half for ten years and you wake up one morning and realize the love has gone. You have become friends; you're simply rubbing along with each other, and not in a good way! There's no spark, the excitement is lost and now it's run of the mill, it's tedious, the conversation flat – a monologue of grunts coupled with irritation, irritation in all they say and do, and you realize this is a relationship that has run its course.

It happens frequently in business; disengagement has taken hold and you no longer believe in what you or the company are trying to achieve. You realize you are no longer bringing your best self and you need to move on, that being the best solution all around.

It might be that something has caught your eye, some-thing that has sparked your attention – another business, another leader, an opportunity for growth, a role with a purpose that's aligned to your values and it's too good to turn down. Whatever your reason to leave, this should be handled with care. You have given ten years of your life to this business; you have added value and you have grown with the organization through the years.

What does the process of leaving look like? What experi-ence has your organization shaped to ensure that this person leaves on a high? How has the business protected this rela-tionship so it doesn't end in a bitter divorce? Culture needs to be protected and you can only do that when the full cycle has been considered and acted on; otherwise it will forever look disingenuous.

We all know that feeling we get when you are handing in your notice. It is never comfortable, and particularly when it comes as a shock. If you have a solid relationship with your line manager and they have created an environment where their time is invested in you as a person, your development and your growth in the business, then it will not be a shock. They already saw that the light has gone out in your eyes. They identified you needed more and either provided you with options or had a very honest conversation where they asked you a series of questions, getting you to open up and talk about where you want to go, your aspirations, the type of organization you would like to be at next, how you think you could make a real difference in a business or the type of role you want to develop into.

Within the work environment this isn't a marriage where two people become disinterested; it is typically just one person here – unless the entire team are disengaged, then watch out... The manager should have their eyes peeled; they should have noticed the nuances, the slight change in behaviour. They should have been able to either reignite that spark or work with you to ensure they can create a solution that fits with you both.

Whatever the reason, the manager has noticed, supported and provided protection, and if D Day comes around, you're dotting the I's and crossing the T's of a long-formed conversation.

A business that invests in the development of a strong employee experience and culture must have the right leadership capability wrapped around it to make it work. Creating an employee roadmap and defining the culture is one step; the next is ensuring that every leader knows and understands how to lead their people not just in alignment with the culture but that they believe in leadership; they recognize their role and lead with integrity.

When you have an open relationship, in the work sense, you will understand the real reason for the employee wanting to leave. Where you haven't, then the reason will be harder to determine. The employee or line manager will complete the Leavers' form, neither acknowledging the real reason is because the manager is sh*t, the job is a total bore, that the pressures of the working day are relentless, the expectations too high, or it's down to a toxic culture; no, it will be put down to pay or opportunity, masking the true reason.

And this is for HR to review, to get to the bottom of the real reasons and this will be telling as to whether you have the right culture in the business or not. HR check your processes, take a look at the Leavers' forms, add 'role offered' and 'pay offered in new role' as a field, add a box asking how many times they have applied to internal opportunities in the last year. Add a box about the journey length from home to the new role. Then remove all these as reasons. The reasons need to be deeper than this. If it is pay, you have the facts with the information you have asked for; if it's travel, you have the facts also and if they have been applying for opportunities they haven't been successful in, then it all ties up. But when it doesn't then the real reason is the one you are looking for. Ask the bold questions. Don't skirt the issue; write in plain terms, for example: 'We are working to achieve a culture of transparency and autonomy. Do you feel this is demonstrated in your area of the business? If not, why not?'

What questions would reveal whether the work you are doing towards creating the target culture is having an effect?

Organizations that know their culture candidly ask this question: 'If this role was available at this salary, would you have stayed within this business?' They have built the relationship to be able to ask the questions that challenge the employee to answer authentically and to provide them with the insights they require. They are reviewing the trends and making adjustments.

The negotiables

Then there are the businesses that go into bidding wars! If someone wants to leave an organization and they have found another job, there was a reason for this. You can't be half pregnant as they say; their head has already been turned, so coming in late to then try and place a sticky plaster over the issue with a lump sum is just that... a sticky plaster, one that will soon fall off. It only shows how the individual had to take a bold step before the business rewarded them benefits. OK, you're leaving; now I will appreciate you. It's weak, it's limp, it shows the business and leadership for what they truly are. They will only be pushed into action when challenged with a threat. Are you that business or are you one that is forthcoming and timely in the reward for your employees' efforts?

Notice periods are some of the most painful months of people's careers. You have mentally checked out, but you have an obligation and want to fulfil that obligation to your current business. For those employees who come to work to do a good job, which is the majority, this is the part that will stay with them. Are you a business that locks them down to a three- or even, god forbid, six-month notice period? One that has decided to make a stance, one that doesn't want to set a precedent, who doesn't want to make it easy for that individual or the other business? You refuse any leeway and damage what might have been ten perfectly great years. You have tried to cling on and why? Control!

The said employee is ignored, cut out of anything new; they are now a spare wheel and therefore of little value. So, they are now working less than ever before, turning up physically but not mentally, and the impact is showing not just in the relationship of that individual and their manager, but also in the team around them. The team are now taking on more than their fair share, and are having to cope with the additional responsibilities. Time is wasted talking about the situation, and for all intents and purposes it would be better if that person had just been allowed to leave. Let everyone move on with dignity.

The value of doing it right, the value of putting the individual first, also means you are putting the team first. If you want a strong team culture, then sit down with the team, agree what needs to be done, where they could add the most value over the notice period, and if the agreed timeframe can be reduced. The whole team is engaged; the whole team can see that you treated that person with the utmost respect and that you have created a space for everyone to feel valued. The team understand how they are going to manage as they have been part of the change.

Sometimes you need leaders to leave

The capability of leaders and managers is intrinsic to the health and wellbeing of the whole team. In your business, how do you respond to this? How important is culture to you, to make the big decisions?

If you're a business that has turned a blind eye to the leader who is recognized for their personal performance but not their skills as a leader, consider the benefit of removing the leader; what do you have? A team that is confident in a business who recognize that people's wellbeing is fundamental. Will they lower the performance? More than likely not. Instead, they will work to fill the gap; the return you get for being the business that identified a problem and dealt with it.

Or face up to it: develop that leader on what is and isn't acceptable when leading a team. Is the performance of one leader more important that the ten people they manage resenting their work, the limitations imposed on them or the feeling of entrapment they might have? Look beyond your world and see the impact it can have on people's lives.

Other reasons for leaving

There are clearly many other ways that someone can leave the business, whether this is down to the individual's performance, conduct or capability. It might be due to an organizational restructure within the business or a redundancy situation; whatever the reason may be, as a business agree who you want to be. Deal with the person and process with dignity. If you want to be seen as a great employer with a great culture, then don't fall at this hurdle. You are dealing with people's lives. You are making decisions that can and undoubtedly will have a huge impact on their personal circumstances. Take the time to understand the person, the situation, and deal with them with care. Great companies leave the doors open for good people to return.

Diversity and inclusion

Diversity and inclusion go hand in hand with the development of a strong culture – one where the focus is on executing the purpose of the business through its people.

As with culture, when you have diversity within the organization you will know it. You can see it and feel it; you will instinctively know if your business sees the value of diversity and actively contributes to a strategy that seeks ways to attract and retain diverse employees.

If there is little diversity within the organization, then question whether this is working for you or what your personal views are. If you don't know what the value of diversity is or how to even approach diversity within the workplace, then be honest about it. You are clearly on a path to wanting to develop your organizational culture so diversity and creating the right approach seems fitting. Being honest allows for the right conversations to take place. What does it mean to you and the senior team? What are the benefits and what steps need to be taken?

A thing to watch out for here is when organizations use hiring for 'cultural fit' in their process. What that has a tendency to mean is that the manager seeks to hire someone who they can get along with. If this is the case, then teams begin to look alike and the values of diversity dissipates. Yes, there should be cultural alignment, but diversity can bring so much more, particularly when the focus is on the goal.

Along with an 'engaged team', racially diverse teams outperform non-diverse teams by 35% (in a study completed in 2019 by ClearCompany). MIT conducted a cognitive study to look at the reasons behind this statistic and the findings were down to three factors:

1. They gave one another roughly equal time to talk.
2. They were sensitive towards each other (even in awkward situations).
3. They included more women, making them more diverse.[7]

Essentially, their behaviour was more considered; from a problem-solving, idea generation and collaboration perspective they were far more effective.

So, before we move onto a diversity and inclusion strategy, it would be more pertinent to ask what this means to you, to the business and particularly the board or senior leadership team? Break this down; how is diversity and the value of diversity perceived in the business? Where is diversity prevalent? Is it in all areas or only within key areas or roles within the business? Is diversity championed by the business or just by one area or person, or not at all?

Next look into the big areas for consideration:

Diversity and inclusion plan: This is your plan to demonstrate what your approach is to provide fair and equitable treatment in all areas, ranging from attraction methods, recruitment, pay, performance management to promotion and talent management. It would clearly have the training mapped out, inclusive of all. If you truly want an inclusive culture, one that embraces diversity, then the training needs

---

[7] ClearCompany, '12 diversity statistics that will make you rethink your hiring decisions', 5 June 2020. Available from https://blog.clear-company.com/12-diversity-hiring-statistics-rethink-your-decisions [accessed 18 January 2021].

to be designed and adopted by all and it may even include what the ambition is, and in some areas targets.

Measures: Within your diagnostics include what diversity measures you have. How do you fare as a business on your gender pay gap? How transparent have you been with this and what measures are in place if there is a requirement to close the gap?

The hiring process: Diversity and cultural fit needs to be considered. Look at the values of the individual and how they are aligned to the values within your business. Look at what diversity can add to the breadth of perception within the team. Likeminded team members will only get you so far; look at what you are missing and introduce diversity for the benefit of broader perspectives and thinking.

Leadership behaviours: Are your leaders inclusive by nature; do you need to spell out what inclusivity means or do your managers already understand it, adopting ways to support everyone? Do they first seek to understand each and every employee and balance inclusivity, the needs of their people with getting the day job done? If not, what development are they receiving as part of their management development?

Opportunities: In some businesses where the capability and understanding of the managers and leaders is great, diversity and inclusion happens by stealth. There is no unconscious bias; promotion is based on ability and potential, not by who is favoured as the boy or girl wonder. The 'boys or girls club' should be long gone. 'Networking events' and ethics should be prominent in all areas, including decision making, fair selection for roles and inclusion in all activities.

If you are in a large organization, then you may already have someone who is allocated responsibility for diversity and inclusion, whose efforts continually build a strategy that centres around education, management practice, analytics, initiatives, and so forth. With global businesses, diversity targets are so much more the norm. Review the effectiveness of where you are against the target. What further needs to take place? Who is leading the way in other businesses and what can you learn from others? Learn from the big players who have committed diversity and inclusion as a business priority. Gap, Accenture and Nestlé all aimed to create an environment that fosters diversity. They have Diversity Academies within their development portfolio, diversity training, defined policies and implemented practices all designed to align the culture and diversity of their business with the diversity of their client base. They understand that this is the foundation for innovation, and a way of being attuned to the world around them.

With the information available to you, review the above and look at it from the top down. Do you have a diversity plan and how aligned is that to your culture? Lead this agenda; be clear on how you want the business to be shaped by its people; be clear on what you want to be known for and educate people. Educate your peers so they know the value in diversity; educate your peers and lead the way.

Socially responsible business

Sincerity. This is my go-to word for social responsibility. Without sincerity at the heart of this discussion then it becomes a list of initiatives. We have Mental Health First Aiders – check. We have scheduled a few charity days – check. We provide funding to a charity of our choice – check. Boom; we are socially responsible. It doesn't matter that we don't recycle, that we use so much fuel our environmental footprint has put a hole in the atmosphere the length and width of the Great Wall of China, in which case what's wrong with a bit of fly-tipping here and there?

No way is that a socially responsible business! If you are a business and corporate social responsibility has been defined as one of your values or it is linked to the culture you are trying to create, then you need to review your agenda with integrity, be sincere to the cause and along with culture don't leave any stone unturned. If you want to be a business that cares, then care and get everyone to care with you.

Being socially responsible means so much more than just advertising charitable initiatives or the annual summer fete fundraising bash. It's about understanding your organizational purpose and coupling what you are trying to achieve with being considerate to the impact you have on the planet and people.

Social responsibility seeps into many areas of the business, whether large, medium or small in scale. In decision making, do your decisions support this agenda or debunk it? Start first by looking at the small, run-of-the-mill business-as-usual activity: recycle bins, double-sided printing, utilization of video calling and minimizing non-essential travel, turning lights off, powering down laptops. Very simple basics but every business can have an impact.

Complete an assessment, break down your social impact into categories, turn on your social consciousness and consider whether you're an organization that is doing things right or whether there is room for improvement. Anchor in someone who has a real passion who can explore all the avenues that your business can look at to review and get them to table short-, medium- and long-term improvements. Gauge how the leadership team wants to steer this ship. At what costs will you become a socially responsible business?

There are many businesses out there leading the way. Lego... who would have thought? Those troublesome foot-endangering pieces of plastic that your littles ones leave scattered around so you have the pleasure of trying to do the muffled swear face are one of the key leaders in corporate social responsibility. A company built on small pieces of plastics managed to quickly hurdle any long-term organizationally damaging criticism over their environmental impact; instead, they set about creating one of the most compelling strategies. In 2018, Lego announced that 2% of their Lego plastic elements were now made from plant-based plastic sourced from sugar cane with an overall ambition to have all their products and packaging made from sustainable materials by 2030.

The business that is built on making plastic toys came top of a 2019 ranking of global companies' reputation for social responsibility organized by the Reputation Institute in the United States, beating Microsoft and Google. This is a business that could have taken a battering; instead, it remodelled itself (excuse the pun!). Lego doesn't just have a social consciousness; it changed its entire business model from top to bottom to build a socially responsible and ethical business that will now withstand the test of time. That's a cultural shift.

If you're a global giant, I assume you have this in hand already. It is likely that you have this agenda represented at board level, that you are challenging yourself on who you are and who you want to be, and from that looking at who you want to work with. There is zero point being an ethical business when your partners or suppliers are operating in ways which are completely unethical. Have you done your homework and does that sit OK with you? Are these the people whose pockets you want to line, or do you need to make some bold choices?

Businesses built with strong ethical purpose aren't doing this for the badge of honour. Instead, they will have built a robust, long-term strategy and are forging their own way. They are leading instead of following, as it's authentic to who they want to be.

If you are a smaller business, then take this time to consider how you are aligning culture with your social responsibility. How far do you want to take it, who owns the agenda and are you sincere to its cause? Don't play with it! This is not a good case for a PR opportunity; make it real.

We have changed globally. The Covid-19 pandemic made people think differently; the social consciousness has been raised within each and every one of us. It is time we all take action; we need to think differently, and no I'm not going all Greta Thunberg on you, but I am urging you to consider two factors that we should all feel strongly about: people and planet.

Dress code

Is this as daft as it seems? What does the dress code (if you have one) say about the culture you have? Staggeringly, there are still organizations that stipulate the length of the 'acceptable skirt' level. 'The skirt must be worn no more than 2 inches above the knee.' For the love of god, who the hell is walking around with a tape measure; is this the role of the receptionist? For the sake of this example, I now liken the receptionist to a 1950s matron. Does said matron sit at the reception desk with their finger hanging heavily over an ejector button? As each new skirt-wearing employee walks in, they eyeball the length of the skirt with the accuracy of a carpenter's laser measure. Without a murmur or movement, the button is pressed, the skirt a full .2 millimetres over the ruling has been poleaxed from the business. The public shaming resulting in the said wearer going home and returning in a full neck-to-floor gown.

Extreme I know, but it's true; OK maybe not the matron bit or the ejector button, but the rule is. Do you think this business is one that embraces innovation, that is forward thinking, or is it stifling and mediocre?

In businesses where there's no dress code, just bring your best self: wear what you deem appropriate for the day you are about to have. If you're with a client and they wear business attire, then wear business attire; if you're having a day in the office collaborating and you want to feel comfortable, be comfortable. This allows everyone to be adult about the choices they make. But if for some unspeakable reason some of the employees start wearing thigh-high boots or looking like they slept in their clothes, then maybe have a chat with them about their own personal brand and how what they are wearing might be perceived by others. Equally, if you have a culture of wearing thigh-high boots and this is a win for the team as it's never been so engaged, then let it rock out. It's your business; it has to be right for you.

Health and safety agenda taken into account, ensure that your people have the necessary PPE(Personal Protective Equipment) and that they wear it. The key to all PPE is that it's best worn on! Your agenda should be one where you want each of your employees to return home safely that day.

In all seriousness, how are you managing the culture of safety within your teams? How do you ensure that each person under your remit is looked after in the physical sense? Using the right equipment and wearing the right kit? What is acceptable if you are allowing visitors or support staff onto a construction site or into a warehouse? Have you determined what is acceptable so that you and everyone knows how to look after their people? Holding people to account isn't difficult, especially when the aim is to keep them free from hurt and, more importantly, alive.

What we wear says a lot about our personality and it speaks volumes about the culture of the organization. Take this into account, talk to your people, find out what threads (see what I did there) will allow them to bring their best self to work and gain complete agreement that this is the step you want to take.

This chapter was written to give you insights from the employee perspective about each stage of the lifecycle. Some obvious, some less so; some obvious, but not always actioned. The importance I place on each thread is for cultural continuity. Only by considering each stage do you create a culture that binds together people, purpose and strategy. Consider each thread and go back to your planning stage: what actions do you want to take to ensure that you have the best chance at creating a culture shift in your business?

6

Threadbare

The impact on culture when stress tested

Culture exposed

The true authentic culture of a business is exposed when it is stress tested or undergoes significant change. Like people, when businesses are faced with adversity it's the response that matters.

When organizations are put under stress and strain, it impacts their core. Their authentic self shines through; decisions will be made based on what is important at that moment in time, decisions will be made quickly and those decisions will have a lasting impact on each and every employee. Your business will be remembered for how you responded.

Whether change is something as significant as the Covid-19 pandemic or a simple office move, we all know how much animosity it can produce. Change should never be underestimated. The impact of change can be significant and never more so than when we are in a place of comfort and then our metaphorical blanket is removed.

Change when there is no acceptance

Change without acceptance is change imposed upon us. Are we suddenly effective? Have we taken the change and run with it? Most likely not.

Regardless of its degree or scale, change requires a level of acceptance. The level of acceptance determines the level of effectiveness. If there is significant change and little acceptance, then there will be little effectiveness. The question here is: How do we get acceptance? And what is the role of the organization? How change is handled will be a clear indicator of the organizational culture and the attitude towards the people who work there.

We have all been in a situation on a night out where someone, maybe you, maybe me, tried to cajole the rest of the group of people to go to the latest hotspot. But half the group don't want to go, two want to go home, four want a curry, and so on. The instigator though is relentless and eventually you're all there; the music is deafening, the atmosphere tepid, the latest hotspot flooded with wannabes and really it's quite dire. As the group disbands, they are already resenting the £10 they had to pay to get in and the second cab of the evening to go back to the place they really wanted to be.

> We tried to make a change; there was no acceptance – it was completely ineffective; actually it was worse, it was damaging. Nick from accounts got so intoxicated he vomited on Mary from payroll, which has now resulted in compete uproar, a grievance and a large amount of time and resource being dedicated to what could have been corrected with the original pleas of food being heard and actioned.

I would like to say the above example is extreme, but that statement alone would be questionable. What was extreme, however, was being faced with a global pandemic. Covid-19 shook the world, an example of change being invoked in a colossal sense on people and businesses. It had an immediate impact on how we worked, our economy, the health and well-being of the world, the resilience of the organization and the employees. It changed how we worked forever.

There were the organizations who were stress tested and folded. Egotistical, they kept an eye only on the commercial impact, the bottom line, the values on the wall now misaligned with the actions they undertook and, ultimately, they suffered because of it.

One organization (Bird) hosted a Zoom call which informed 406 employees that they were not to return to work from Monday onwards. That an email would follow that would provide those affected with details of their severance. They then focused the call largely on how the IT kit of those employees would need to be returned. For those who didn't get on the Zoom call, they only found out that they had lost their jobs from another colleague or when the email landed in their inbox. Not only did this business suffer bad press, but they lost talent who I dare say won't return should the opportunity ever arise in the future.

There were organizations who strived in the chaos, not just in a commercial sense but also in a cultural sense. They had already created a culture that could flex, that was people oriented; the values, the bedrock of the business, remained the same. As these organizations were stress tested, they weathered the storm and kept true to their culture. They appreciated the impact and significance of this on their colleagues and their country.

How did your organization fare? Were you one that made the early decisions to introduce home working, established new working practices and supported your people in the change curve? Or did you try to operate as long as possible before the public pressure became too great?

Change when there is acceptance

The Covid-19 pandemic and the change incurred here was an external event. It could never have been prepared for but change in any business happens continually. If you have a culture of delivering change effectively then you already know the impact on people and you are prepared for that. You know and understand the steps needed to engage your people on the journey. These increase their level of acceptance and you have an engaged community because of it.

Where a business creates change and acknowledges that the change impacts people, they create a plan to ensure that they land the change effectively. By doing so, they can increase the level of acceptance, which ultimately delivers the right results for the business.

Change with acceptance is a different ball game. We have accelerated towards the end goal, all because we're there! The leader has explained the why; we saw the value, the benefit and we adapted because of it. Instead of being done to, we became 'part' of the change.

Change plan

In business, when there is change – for example, a new system implementation, new processes or new reporting lines – nine times out of a ten there is a plan, a business plan, a list of actions that need to take place, by whom and when. What's typically missing is a well-thought-through 'Change People Plan'. A plan that looks at how the change will impact people, a stakeholder analysis breaking down the change impact and appropriate communication methods to inform the stakeholder populations, the testing log, training that needs to be delivered and to whom, awareness to ensure that the implementation is accepted and the process to sign off from an employee impact... and breathe.

In large-scale projects, the implications of not doing this well are that productivity will suffer, political game playing will become prevalent, commercial profits will suffer. The change – a new system, new processes, new structure, redundancy situation; they will all be criticized. Time will be lost; there will be disengagement, and costs will be impacted. Enabling business change though focusing on increasing acceptance increases productivity, morale and engagement. Organizations that do this really well recognize that a small change to some may have major consequences on others; we all have very different perceptions of change.

How does your business ease the change process? How are the decisions made aligned with the values and the culture you want?

The Covid-19 pandemic was a great example that we should explore – it provided so much intelligence on the culture of businesses. This was a global stress test like no other. Consider the actions your business took in the areas described in the following text. How aligned were your actions to the culture you want, the values you have, and did your actions give you the results you needed?

The home-working trend

Office workers were instructed to work from home. For the home workers and agile workers out there already, the change impact was little, but for those who had never worked in physical isolation before, how did you support them in making that change? Did you provide them with the physical tools and mental preparation? Were the line managers equipped with the skills and understanding on how to manage virtual teams and were expectations on deliverables re-aligned, considering the change and the time it would take to make the adjustment?

Leading remote teams comes with new challenges, virtual one-to-ones, although distanced, do allow for concentrated time for your manager to engage with their employee without the distraction of the workplace. Was guidance provided to managers to support them in the move to remote leadership? Was the outline of how people should operate in this new world provided and the support given to help the mental shift? Where businesses faced into the reality of the new way of working, there was an appreciation that people were anxious. A new form of stress was prevalent; this, coupled with the isolation of remote working, needed handling gently.

Employee wellbeing

How active were you as a business in pushing the health and wellbeing agenda? Did you face up to the anxiety this was causing people and provide direct access to gain the support they needed? Did you take the time to support your team with the transition? Did you acknowledge the degree of human connection that was lost and take action to provide them with the human connection they needed?

If you had a clear virtual communication approach and technology readily available, was this a simple process? Team conference calls established. A morning call, to check in, to see how everyone was feeling and a light touch on what were the priorities, acknowledging these would change daily based on external pressures.

Through any change, keeping in touch is an essential part of showing the team that you are there for them, to provide focus and to allow for questions to be asked. Most importantly, it's to provide connection, a way to ensure you can see how the impact of the change is affecting your team and for you to have the emotional insight to help them adjust.

Processes

New processes needed to be created quickly. Where demand on supply became great or where businesses completely diversified their product range, how agile was your business to adjust? The supply chain needed to move quicker; new behaviours in handling needed to be introduced; social distancing in warehousing challenged the increase in demand on supply. There were new processes in supermarkets; kiosks were installed to protect the employees, markings to ensure social distancing and then the role of the employee was to police and challenge those who were not taking caution. Supermarkets had to change the role of security; they now had bouncers. Did anyone else feel like they had regressed somewhat, standing in a queue at some dismal sweaty club on a Saturday night, waiting desperately to catch the eye of the doorman to let you in? Roles changed in so many ways and people's behaviours had to follow suit.

How was the red tape removed? Accountability had to be increased to allow for decisions to be made quickly. What processes had to be stopped to ensure efficiencies were being applied? How did you communicate on each of the changes, how did you maintain focus on what was taking place or not taking place while maintaining wellbeing, and did you keep explaining the why? Did you provide your people with the context of changes, so they understood the bigger impact and were able to piece the jigsaw together, allowing for an increase in acceptance?

Dyson, one of the first to diversify, worked to meet the needs of the government and the NHS to design and create ventilators that were so desperately needed. They were a front-runner in this step to support; they led where others then followed.

The team knew their purpose; they understood the why and became a critical factor in the wellbeing of the nation.

They needed to be an intricate part of the wheel that was required to save lives. The pressure felt must have been great, but to understand the why, to understand the context and to see your product helping so many can only drive a team to effectiveness. This alone shows how capable we are to diversify, to flex when the leadership and personal motivation is driving you towards a cause that was a landmark in our history.

Burberry followed and diversified, moving their workforce to make hospital gowns and fast-tracking 100,000 face masks from their Yorkshire factory. They provided funding to the University of Oxford for vaccine research along with contributing to two charities tackling food poverty.

Consider the cultures that were fast to move and whether this was similar to your own business.

Techucation (technology education)

Overnight, the entire world became more technically savvy, with video calling and conference calling the norm. Digital platforms rose in popularity and are here to stay. The online pub quiz which rippled through the nation showed that we can still be connected and made all the less known tools the norm.

We changed. Not only because we developed new skills; we multi-tasked in ways we never knew possible; we learnt to appreciate the smaller things in life. We slowed down, we took stock, we spring cleaned, we noticed the change in seasons, we learnt to play, we learnt to educate our children, we learnt to care more about people and the world and less about things that used to keep us awake at night that no longer seemed important. We changed.

What we learnt about culture

There were some unscrupulous organizations; those that took this as an opportunity for an excuse to complete their annual cull. A reason that was an external excuse to leverage the annual cost-cutting routine. These were the organizations that will be remembered and talked about, the ones that will suffer long term as their true culture came to the fore.

There were businesses that didn't survive the pressures and had to close their doors, some that were transparent and that supported and guided their employees step by step. Those that treated their employees so well that, should they ever be in a position to reopen their doors, the employees left in a way that would have them returning. And then there were those that didn't and will be remembered for a culture no one wants to be part of.

There were businesses who survived that didn't support their teams' transition, and with little or no support they delayed the period of performance, lowered the level of output and created further ambiguity.

These were the organizations that didn't evolve that went on to remove the ability to work remotely and reimplemented 100% attendance back in the office as soon as they could. Trust broken. When the elasticity of people's skill has been tested, which it had, then why would you allow it to snap back to how it was before? Keep exercising their new skills, allow them to use it, trust in your people and reap the rewards of having new and developed skills. To return to as it was before is to unwittingly say that you didn't trust their performance during the most challenging time. That it wasn't good enough.

There were leaders who stood out – the empathic leaders, the ones who supported their teams, whose motivation was to bring their tribe through it and to come out stronger for it. They built personal and team resilience; they continued to drive results for the business, but through the enablement and support they wrapped around their team members. The thinking time and effort that surrounded the transition will have endless benefits.

Organizations that have a strong culture of change and the methodology in place to increase acceptance, these organizations moved quicker, innovated faster, and all because the employees understood why and have trust in their leadership.

As with all things relating to change, it's not the change that always matters. This isn't just about the pandemic: it is about all things change related that impact people. When the process has been developed that wraps its arms around you, that shows that what you're doing is fair, then you will succeed. Acceptance accelerated, buy-in gained and adoption of a new world is then soon within grasp.

Change in your business

As a business, how do you handle change? After change has been implemented, do you complete a lessons learnt? Do you share it with the business, with every single employee? If in hindsight you got it wrong, do you explain why and if you have gone back on those decisions, did you explain and own it? Change is a prime opportunity to show:

- Your employees that you are a human – that as a business you're willing to learn and evolve.
- That recovery is the best and only solution; ignorance to when change has been handled badly will only demonstrate that you are no longer interested in the impact it had and that you have moved on. Your employees, however, won't; they will be scarred and impacted long after the change. It is the duty of the business to help their employees move forward with guidance and support.
- Build on the change: remote working and techucation are examples where new skills were developed – harness the new skills, the agile workforce and the resilience developed and build a stronger culture for it.

Organizations who handle change effectively with their people will thrive and rebuild faster than their competitors.

They are the businesses that know that the role of the manager continually changes. The manager/leader of tomorrow is not the manager/leader of today. They are the managers who can lead agile teams, who connect the disconnected (physically), who have the emotional intelligence to recognize that performance is a clear indicator of their own leadership. They are managers who understand stress that derives from change, what the stress indicators are, how underlying stress can have a damaging imprint and how to help guide their people through the daily challenges that might impact.

The Covid-19 pandemic was a period in time where people saw suffering; people supported each other in the most admirable way and sadly there was loss. We all felt it. How do you rebuild with a stronger culture than you had before? What lessons did you take from such significant change that allowed you to realign who you want to be as a business?

Organizations that shone in the pandemic had true authentic cultures; like the phoenix that rises from the ashes, they took full opportunity to learn about how they handled it. They recognized that every single person had been impacted and that each person's view of the world has undoubtedly shifted. They acknowledged that this was a time to create a new norm. They celebrated the behaviours of those who have taken the mantle and performed, the natural leaders who stepped up in the face of adversity. They looked at the business they were before and the one they want to become, and they took action.

When you are defining the culture you want, review every inch, review your moral compass, hold up a mirror to the entrenched behaviours as this is the time where an honest conversation needs to be had about what type of business you want to be recognized as. It is not your strategy or purpose that people will know you for, but how you treated your people.

Creating effective change

I will explore this at a broad level as there are far greater experts out there in the field of change. I will, however, provide it in the context of how change, or should I say, the handling of change, can impact culture and/or define it.

It is also pertinent to point out that when you are creating a 'cultural development programme' you are involving change, so in itself the handling of how you create the change will either support your agenda or damage it.

The change curve

Let's start with how the process of change can affect us. At some point in all our lives we will have been through the change curve, the suite of emotions (denial, anger, bargaining, depression and finally acceptance) we go through when change is imposed on us.

Now we all know we are not all the same. There are the extremes, such as:

- **Lovers of change**: Throw change at them and it's great, it's exciting, it's a welcome break to a monotonous day. They thrive off the energy.
- **Creators of change**: They make change part of daily practice, purely so they can feed off it. They crave the drama, fuelled by the focus and the short-term accomplishments. They are undoubtedly so task focused that they forget the day job is still there.
- **Change loathers**: It sickens them; they have their routine and this is disruption. It may be that they have been exposed to change in their past that was executed so poorly it has left an imprint that is triggered by all future change. These employees will take much longer to get to acceptance and, whatever their reason, your purpose is to engage, to listen, to explain why, rationalize and help them to make a paradigm

shift to see that this change can be done well and it will be for the long-term good.

When imposing change or having change imposed on us, we have to remember there are 7.8 billion people on this planet and not one of them sees the world in the way that you do. Your upbringing, your education, the beliefs and experiences you have gained through your years, shape how you see the world and not a single person can mirror that. Change is personal; be considerate to the fact that whatever your view is on change, or the view of the business, it is not the view of each and every person it impacts. That's what makes us great – our differences. But it is also what makes change increasingly challenging.

The Kübler-Ross Change Curve, also known as the five stages of grief, has become widely adapted in varying forms to show the stages of emotions which a person undergoes when impacted by grief, or by the impact of significant change.[1]

The five stages are denial, anger, bargaining, depression and acceptance.

With the Covid-19 pandemic as an example, we all went through the change curve, some of us spending longer in some stages than others. Initially, *Denial*; we saw what was happening in China but at the very beginning many of us didn't think it would impact our country.

Then it became real; we started hearing that schools were to close, people were to self-isolate, the bulk buying went extreme as fear gripped the country: *Anger*. People were angry about what was happening, the selfishness that was in full flight, angry about the economic impact, the impact it would have on us directly, our jobs, our livelihoods. It all become real, but then we started *Bargaining*; for those of us with children, we were arguing with ourselves as to what was the best option for our children: close schools, keep them

---

[1] E. Kübler-Ross, *On Death & Dying*. Scribner, 1969.

open? We saw the government bargaining, news and advice coming out and then being retracted, they themselves going through the process and trying to guide each UK country to the best outcome as quickly as possible.

Then we moved into *Depression*, sadness or fear, sometimes shown as indifference, the point of no return. Self-isolation impacted people in solitary confinement, jobs were lost, businesses crippled, government help was advised but the access to the information needed hard to navigate and then there was an overload of news. Social media was a pandemic information takeover, there was no escape from it, and to top it off we still couldn't find a bleeding toilet roll! We needed to find a new way to live; we needed to move forward and find a way through, to keep our hope.

Then finally the last stage, *Acceptance*; this is where we realized we were fighting a change that was not going away and eventually we became resigned to the situation. But more than the fact that there was a change, our behaviour, the way we lived our lives, changed. We video called, we held virtual pub quizzes, we laughed again, we re-connected, we saw light, we saw the rainbows in the windows, we appreciated the peace, the time we had that allowed us to think, to connect back with our own thoughts, our dreams, things that had been packed away for so long. And finally, we looked forward; we looked forward to a time where we could truly appreciate the world in all its glory again.

Covid-19 wasn't a change we wanted nor one we were prepared for, but it had impacted our lives. Our world had all of a sudden been turned upside down and somehow we reached a level of acceptance. We accepted a new norm, a new way of life; one we had never experienced before.

We cannot choose to blindly ignore the impact change has on an individual. We all have our paradigms of the world – a way we look at it with our filters. What may not be a challenge in one person's world may very well be someone else's Mount Everest.

A methodology for change

For any business change programme, whether a pandemic, a restructure or a change due to business growth, there needs to be a methodology to change, one that looks at the impact of the people affected and is consistently applied to each change programme. The reason why is to ensure consistency. Consistency of approach will determine the culture you have. Equally, the culture you have will determine the effectiveness of the change.

If we go back to the Competing Values Framework, the values *Collaborate* and *Control* are internally focused; naturally, these are the cultures that are people centric and therefore there's an expectation that these businesses do change well.

The *Create* and *Control* cultures are externally focused and therefore there is a natural assumption that change may not be handled as well as it could be. *Create* has the advantage of working towards a common purpose; however, this is an environment that suits all. *Control* also due to its competitive nature might see speed of attack taking priority over how any change imposed impacts the employees within the business.

Knowing the culture you are in and the culture you want to become, you have already devised a plan. We have acknowledged change is ever present, so continuity of how you design and implement your change methodology will ensure that you remain consistent with the culture you are trying to create.

Things to consider

Looking at your organization, when change is imposed, whether internal or external, how do you handle the human effect of change on your employees?

Your change methodology needs to be reviewed in line with your business. It may be that it's an internal programme that has developed over years, or it might be one that is backed by all the years of research and behavioural change science. Does the methodology provide you with the measures of success: time, budget, business objectives, technical and human objectives? Whichever methodology you have, you need to consider if it is right for your culture and whether it enhances your culture. Consider the following:

- **Flexibility**: Does the methodology you use give you the flexibility you need? Many known frameworks are linear in their approach. These are useful for some businesses but not for others.
- **Choice**: Does your framework allow you to be selective with the tactics? Can you choose what you need based on your current change or do you want a road map of all activity that *must* be applied every time?
- **Consistency**: Is the framework known by everyone and used consistently because it's effective?

Your change methodology will only ever be as good as it is used. Review it, but equally review its application.

Take a look at key projects and delve into the detail. With each decision that was made, was there an impact review? What did the plan cover to help your employees through the change curve? What development is provided for leaders who go through the same change curve? How does the business accelerate this so the leader can focus on supporting others?

Consider whether what you have is fit for purpose or, in light of the culture you want to see in the business, consider how you can create a methodology that works for you. Build a process; build a communication plan, a decision-making guide; build a way to protect the leaders and decision makers in ensuring their oxygen masks are fitted before they try to fit the mask of others. Look at ways that allow for more of the business to support in the decision making. Identify your foot soldiers, those who advocate change, and bring them in. Bring them in now and listen to how the change has impacted employees and the business in all areas and build ways to improve. Acknowledge the learnings and implement a culture that enables your employees to transition smoothly when faced with adversity.

Define how you want to manage change going forward and share this with the business. This will not just happen; it is change in itself. Educate your people on the psychology of change and the value it brings when change is executed well. Reap the benefits of increased productivity, and engaged teams, the sense of community.

This is the definition of cultural development. When change occurs, it applies pressure onto a business and its people. Help your teams to weather the storm and learn from it; evolve your approach through listening to those impacted and learn ways in which to improve and share with everyone. It is a continual cycle, as is change. Get it right, or at least show you want to, and you remain authentic; mask over the mistakes and you will lose the faith and trust of your teams.

The pressures of change in any form strip the organization of its cloth; when we are threadbare, we are vulnerable in the truest of words. It is only then, ego removed, our true self, that organizationally we know that the culture we curated is the true culture.

7

Over to you

You picked up this book because the culture of your organization is critical to your business success. It is the only commodity you have in business that can make your company unique; everything else can be replicated. But the rationale as to why culture should be tabled goes much deeper than being unique. It should part of a leader's DNA; the desire to build a better future for all. A company that improves lives through the products or services supplied to the end consumer, through the environment you create; a company with the desire to improve the lives of the people who make that happen. Your employees.

This book provides you with some guided steps. If you are choosing to work through these then through the process first identify whether you as a business have psychological safety in place for your teams to be honest about your current culture.

Challenge the level of transparency in your business and question the implication of this. What do you need to first change, for your people to face up to this wholeheartedly and give you the honesty you need to grow the culture of your business?

Show you mean business; take a bold step and show that you're willing to listen. Acknowledge that change can only happen when people can speak up without fear of reprimand. Boldness in this step alone will show that a new dawn is coming. Cultural development is hard and small discrete steps will not move the mountain...

With psychological safety in place, allow people to show up; give them the space and the right tools to be honest about your culture and to determine whether the culture is the right one for your business. Gather your data and make sense of it. Take time to reflect on what has worked so far and at what cost.

It is worth pointing out that you are not alone. Our workplace culture has become one where we value results and for many people this has been at the cost of their health, wellbeing and in some cases the cost of their families – precious lost time or the impact of the stress from the day seeping into an unpleasant evening or worse.

If there was ever a more compelling reason for cultural development

Let's put this all into some perspective: around 32 million people aged 16 and over go into a workplace every day. We spend on average 3,507 days at work in a lifetime and we consider quitting our jobs 16 times a year.[1] Couple this with the mental health crisis. In the UK alone, Mind have suggested that approximately one in four people in the UK will experience a mental health issue each year.[2] A major cost contributor to a business. Identify the financial implications

[1] G. Bailey, 'British people will work for average of 3,507 days over a lifetime, survey says'. *The Independent*, 26 September 2018. Available from www.independent.co.uk/life-style/british-people-work-days-lifetime-overtime-quit-job-survey-study-a8556146.html?amp [accessed 8 January 2021].

[2] Mind, *Mental Health Facts and Statistics*, 2017. Available from www.mind.org.uk/media-a/2958/statistics-facts-2017.pdf [accessed 8 January 2021].

of wellbeing within your own organization, along with the financial reasons for ensuring wellbeing, and then look at the moral obligation of being a business leader.

Look at your moral obligation to your people with serious intent. If each business looked deeply at the culture within their organization and took a realistic look at the impact it has and the effect of their actions on the health and wellbeing of those they employed, how might this help the silent pandemic that has been growing in the background – mental health?

Before you head into the detail of the typical 'HR cycle of events', the performance reviews, the employee opinion surveys, the forums, ask yourselves one question: 'Are we proud of the way we treat all of our employees?' Ask others; ask it with the sincerity this question deserves and answer it with your whole heart. There are some amazing organizations out there that will be able to answer this wholeheartedly and those are the organizations that are great in their own right – commercially sound, attractive businesses whose culture is aligned with the true intent and purpose of what they set out to achieve. A culture of inclusivity and a culture where the employees feel safe.

But for those organizations or those teams where the question was asked and you waivered, where the simple word 'yes' was withheld, then question what in today's society you can do to make this business good enough to protect your people.

And by protect I don't mean ticking the employment law box, understanding what's right and what's wrong, what's legally acceptable and what's not. This is no longer enough. Your spiralling costs will continue at an alarming rate and this is business. Challenge the people costs, look at the impact of lost productivity and start aligning it with damaging behaviours.

Look at the role of HR. Have they become a function, a team or a person managing the tactical elements that is now all consuming? What do you need from this function to drive the people agenda? Is their strategy one that is pushing the business forward or along the way have they become one that is holding you back?

Review your process, the environment that has been inadvertently holding you back and what you can change to accelerate you forward.

Who do you want to be?

Then look at who you want to be. Successful businesses recognize that true collaboration comes when people feel safe. Safe to share, safe to give feedback, safe to try and fail without fear of reprimand. Creating this environment will give you everything you need to drive the business forward. Your team will tell you what will work, what will not and what more could be achieved.

When self-limiting beliefs are removed, so is the ceiling on innovation. Look at your leaders, their ability and what behaviours they model. The culture of your business is only an image reflection of what they do.

Organizationally, look at your employees, look at the leaders and see whose beat of the drum they are beating to. Are they beating to the drum of the business in a way you want, or have they gone wayward?

Then explore deeply whether your leaders are creating the culture for your teams to thrive. Do your leaders know their own conscious and subconscious needs; do they have that level of self-awareness? Only when they have can they really know how to best serve their employees.

Subconscious needs – We can see what is happening at a conscious level, but the real value comes when leaders go below the conscious level. That's when they access the stuff that really matters. These are the influencing thoughts that determine behaviour. Behaviour that determines culture.

We are operating in a time where change is fast and unsurmountable in business and in life itself, change which is continually impacting people. When leaders recognize this and explore what is going on subconsciously in response to an imposed change, they see beyond the action and challenge the deeper impact. They are the leaders that have the conversations that really matter.

They take the time to delve into the real reasons of what's causing the internal and sometimes external conflict; they work to unmask the real issue. They explore the reason, not the reaction, and then they help their teams to overcome the deeper issues.

They recognize that we don't know what we don't give ourselves time to consider.

Why wellbeing is paramount

Start right now

The time is now. Decide what you want the culture of the business to be. Start with yourself: are you the leader you want to be? Identify your gaps, talk to your team about the leader you want to be and ask how close you are to being that leader – what attributes do you have and what do you not? Allow your team to shape you; this is not weakness, this is power.

If you can be honest with your team and provide them with a framework for feedback, you can develop your personal growth. Will it be easy? *No.* Will it be comfortable? *Absolutely not.* But we grow most when we step out of our area of comfort. Take direct action about what you want to do, the leader you want to become for your people. You can then work with your team to collectively decide how you want to be with each other, defining the boundaries of what is and isn't acceptable. Defining the team you want to become and then breaking down the steps you need to take. You are starting to change the culture.

When you are really honest, you already know the answers; you know which behaviours are off and then you forgive the behaviour due to the value their performance brings. Is it right? If people within your business, your team, are causing people undue stress, then is this right? At what cost is this to the culture you are trying to create? And what will be the long-term impact on your business and the people within it? These are the big questions you need to ask.

The Covid-19 pandemic forced inner reflection, a time for those who took great pleasure in going inwards, asking themselves the more meaningful questions around whether what they were doing in life aligned with their deeper sense of purpose. Or they simply appreciated time at home, the slog becoming less so, the Sunday night blues replaced with a solid good night's sleep. They spent more time with family, the opportunity of being at home to see their new baby roll over, which they would have missed otherwise.

And then there will be those who took discomfort from this time of reflection, those with a more extraverted personality who longed for interaction, who missed their colleagues and the office as though it were an extension of themselves, but they too would have found a new way of working. Some longed for the days to be back as they once were but that will never happen: the world has changed, your people have changed, and your processes will undoubtedly have to change forever more.

This is your time to review how you fared. How did you really do as a business or as a leader in your treatment of your people? What did you learn from what happened and, more importantly, what learnings will you take from it? Senior leaders in all organizations found a new way of working, they will be behaving differently, and your culture will change because of it. How your leaders behave is the culture itself. Consciously, are the new behaviours the ones you want the culture to be? And are the behaviours reflected in your company values? What needs to be changed?

As a business, look at your investment and see if it is fairly distributed to ensure that you are serving everyone in the right way. Are you developing the products and services for your customers in the same balance as you do for your own people? How committed are you to ensuring that you are hiring people who have a growth mindset, those people whose natural curiosity allows them to approach each challenge with the open-mindedness it deserves? You don't need people who know the answers because their answers are all already shaped, formed, from another time, or from another company. Yes, that knowledge is great but open-mindedness and curiosity allow for an approach each time that provides the solution for now... in today's context, in your business, no one else's.

Look at the development you provide. Is it the right development that drives the culture though? Are people hungry to evolve, are you providing them with the resources, the tools, that ignite that hunger and give them what they need to be the leaders and subject-matter experts that will see your business thrive?

What are you doing to ensure that the people within your business are building it up and not pulling it down? Maybe not overnight, but over time.

The future

What if this became part of the school curriculum? Mental wellbeing is there already; we teach our kids ways to protect their mental health so they have coping strategies, preventative measures. But what if we also educated them on what a successful organization is and how the culture of the organization created its success, a culture that was inclusive, that had the wellbeing of the employee at the heart and that defined an employee journey where people felt connected and belonged.

Imagine this was part of the curriculum; that every new starter knew what a 'great organization' looked like and the steps that the business would take to ensure their employees were looked after; that they knew that their expectation of leadership was one where trust was there from the off, and fear of failure would never come to mind, as they would be protected to try and fail while they took the steps needed to learn. Would we strive to change our ways? Would we invest time into that person as though they have equal importance to our customers? Would we know what was acceptable and what wasn't and would leaders challenge any conflicts in behaviour as the underlying factor remained: our people matter.

There is a change in the landscape, there are new generations who want more, who work with purpose, who want to work in organizations that will serve them equally. They know the difference between mediocracy and excellence; they know what they want. Look through their eyes and see if your company stands up to what they expect. If it does, then you have a partnership that will go far; you have aligned behaviours and vision. If it doesn't, then have a rethink, be honest; work with the new generations and learn from them.

If your business is already successful, then undoubtedly you have everything in place to ensure that it remains that way. If it's successful because you have met a need that was needed, do not fall short of recognizing that there will be a competitor chasing your tail. Someone behind you, ready to take your place. What sets you apart and keeps you ahead of the curve is having a culture where every single employee is behind you metaphorically but ahead of you in their thinking.

Take the ceiling off your people; give people freedom to think, give them the courage to take risks. Lead with integrity so that should they fail in their ideas, you're behind them supporting them and educating them on how you fail fast.

Talk to your teams about what you want but explain the *why*; explain why it is so important that we start looking at the people agenda, not because HR have told us to but because we want to be part of a movement that changes the land-scape. Paint the picture of how you want everyone to feel when they leave work each day and how you want them to feel each morning before they start their working day.

Leadership is crucial to the ongoing success of culture; only bring in leaders who will work to your agenda. Know what you want because you have done the groundwork. Know that your biggest investment in culture is in the leaders who present it.

And finally

There is so much information out there that I hope this book provided you with time for reflection and questions to ask yourself and the business you are in. I hope that this forms part of a blueprint of what steps you could take.

Be brave about what you are trying to achieve and where the gaps in the current world are. And challenge anyone and everyone on the importance of culture and the value placed in it.

Cost up your losses and map your cultural indicators so that you have a steer; establish monthly dialogue to show the ongoing cost that is hitting or saving the business. Make it tangible – this is not a pink and fluffy activity that requires great posters; this is the soul of your organization that you are looking at. The heartbeat, what matters and what doesn't, and if people don't matter then nor will your business or customers to your people.

Then reap the benefits: watch innovation come to life, see engagement with your own eyes, trial no email Fridays or post 4pm, trial ideas that your employees recommend and watch them make them work. If they want them to, nothing will stop them.

The power of culture is vast. Long have we lived in cultures, in neighbourhoods, in communities, in tribes. Create one in your business that people talk about for the right reasons. Instil pride into your business; be proud of your people and take a step back. When you have teams of people who want to be there for you, for your team or your business, the strength of what you can do and how far you can go is boundless.

Be responsible and own that responsibility. People are fragile; make sure that your people can bare their souls to you, that each day they bring their true self. Help them remove the masks, the armour that people have fitted while trying to fit in. Become a business that asks for progress, not perfection. Progress that takes place each day, small incremental steps that each person takes and is rewarded for.

This is your golden thread, the continual thread that links each interaction the employee has with the culture you are trying to create. Entwine the thread with deep purpose and strategy and keep the process of cultural development alive, forever on the table.

Be part of the movement. #Culturecreator

About the author

Leanne Hamley is an experienced leader and business coach specializing in behavioural change, leadership development and organizational culture. Having worked across multiple sectors, industries and countries, she understands what makes people and organizations thrive.

She has set up numerous high-performing learning and development functions and has worked on international HR change programmes for major companies such as DHL and Celesio (now McKesson). Her time in Sri Lanka working on a change programme to integrate child Tamil soldiers into a Sinhalese orphanage helped her understand fully the power of culture for behavioural change.

Leanne has now stepped out of the corporate world to follow her passion for developing organizational culture. In 2020 she set up the company Culture Creator, a business designed to help organizations create authentic cultures that put the wellbeing of their people at the heart of the business and where values have real meaning and purpose. Leanne also recently co-founded her second company, 'Wot the Book!' – a personal and professional development podcast series and full membership subscription service.

Acknowledgements

I am hugely grateful for this experience. It was never in my plan to write a book, but now I have I can only be grateful for a career in HR that has allowed me to shape my thinking into some semblance of order with the incredible help of the Practical Inspiration Publishing team.

So thank you to Alison Jones and her team at Practical Inspiration Publishing, together with Katie Finnegan and Lizzie Evans, in giving me deadlines (I almost kept to), art work (I loved) and thorough challenge and advice (I wholeheartedly needed) to create *The Golden Thread*.

The Golden Thread has been shaped by my experiences from within each organization I have been part of; by the businesses of clients I have worked with; and by every leader, good or bad I have been exposed to. You have all taught me something: the impact of culture, the value it can add, the critical nature of leadership and the impact this has on people. Without this, I would never have become as passionate as I am about the experiences an employee enjoys or suffers through; nor would I have written about it with the desire to help organizations become places where people thrive, so thank you.

On a more personal note, Luke, I'll be forever in your debt for introducing me to Kate; I know you probably regret it daily as you now can't shake me off, but thank you. Kate, we met virtually and you have been an incredible cheerleader throughout this entire process. You generously gave me your time and you instilled confidence in my writing that my English teacher never achieved. You have become a brilliant friend and now business partner on our side hustle. You offered so much with your solid advice and experience so thank you; you are the tonic to my gin!

To my peers and old colleagues (Jim, Sarah, Jenny, to name a few), who gave up your time to read extracts and to provide your viewpoints, your encouragement and support was so appreciated. And to those who also provided endorsements, I was, and always will be, blown away; I am forever in your debt – your kindness was overwhelming.

Friends and family, thank you for all your support although I am sure that in light of my ramblings, lockdown was probably a wanted break for some so you could escape me. But to Andrea, who I forced into running with me, a huge thank you. You have had to hear about this book, my trials and tribulations, and yet your support has always been incredible.

And to the three men in my life… you are everything to me.

Matt, thank you for being there for me. Your support is endless and your tolerance very high. Thank you; you earnt your stripes listening, supporting and encouraging me every step of the way.

To my boys, Tate and Buddy, the epitome of distraction in the workplace. I have loved spending lockdown with you. You are two very incredible boys. I hope in some way this book helps organizations shape cultures that pave the way for cultures to be created to allow you to thrive.

CPSIA information can be obtained
at www.ICGtesting.com
Printed in the USA
JSHW051640060621
15476JS00004BA/15

9 781788 602662